Lucy Moore is part of BRF's Barnabas children's ministry team and the Messy Church leadership team, developing Messy Church across the UK and abroad. She is an Associate Missioner for Fresh Expressions and has written a number of other books for BRF including The Gospels Unplugged *(2002),* The Lord's Prayer Unplugged *(2004)* Messy Church *(2006),* Messy Church 2 *(2008) and* All-Age Worship *(2010).*

Text copyright © Lucy Moore 2004
Illustrations copyright © Francis Blake 2004
The author asserts the moral right
to be identified as the author of this work

Published by
The Bible Reading Fellowship
15 The Chambers, Vineyard
Abingdon OX14 3FE
United Kingdom
Tel: +44 (0)1865 319700
Email: enquiries@brf.org.uk
Website: www.brf.org.uk
BRF is a Registered Charity

ISBN 978 1 84101 262 9
First published 2004
Reprinted 2010
10 9 8 7 6 5 4 3 2 1
All rights reserved

Acknowledgments
Unless otherwise stated, scripture quotations are taken from the Contemporary English Version of the
Bible published by HarperCollins Publishers, copyright © 1991, 1992, 1995 American Bible Society.

Scripture quotations taken from the *Holy Bible, New International Version*, copyright © 1973, 1978, 1984
by International Bible Society. Used by permission of Hodder & Stoughton Limited. All rights reserved.
'NIV' is a registered trademark of International Bible Society. UK trademark number 1448790.

p. 104 Text message Lord's Prayer reproduced with kind permission of the Ship of Fools txt msg Lord's
Prayer competition. Website: www.shipoffools.com

p. 104 Pidgin English Lord's Prayer reproduced with kind permission. Source: Matthew Tell Bout Jesus,
Hawaii Pidgin Style, 1997. New York: American Bible Society. Contributed by Mr Grimes, Mrs Grimes
and Viveka Velupillai. Wycliffe Bible Translators US.

Performance and copyright
The right to perform *The Lord's Prayer unplugged* drama material is included in the purchase price, so long
as the performance is in an amateur context, for instance in church services, schools or holiday club
venues. Where any charge is made to audiences, written permission must be obtained from the author,
who can be contacted through the publishers. A fee or royalties may be payable for the right to perform
the script in that context.

A catalogue record for this book is available from the British Library

Printed in Singapore by Craft Print International

The Lord's Prayer unplugged

A wealth of ideas opening up the prayer in ten sessions

Lucy Moore

For Andrew and Gideon Hall,
because otherwise I'll never hear the last of it,
in memory of teatime.
With much love as ever.

Thanks especially to...
*Katie Caine for all your invaluable help; Hollie, Alice, Judith, Alexander, Courtney,
Charlotte, Hannah, Claire, Niamh, Stephen and Richard for your enthusiasm; Sue for the
original idea and impetus; Heather and Carol; and Barbara for words of wisdom.*

*Our Father in heaven
Hallowed be your name
Your kingdom come
Your will be done on earth as in heaven.
Give us today our daily bread
And forgive us our sins as we forgive those who sin against us.
Lead us not into temptation
But deliver us from evil.
For the kingdom, the power and the glory are yours, now and for ever.
Amen*

*Our Father who art in heaven
Hallowed be thy name.
Thy kingdom come,
Thy will be done on earth as it is in heaven.
Give us this day our daily bread
And forgive us our trespasses as we forgive them that trespass against us.
And lead us not into temptation
But deliver us from evil.
For thine is the kingdom, the power and the glory, for ever and ever.
Amen*

Contents

Teach us to pray

 Peter nudged John. 'So what's Jesus got that I haven't?' he asked. John thought a moment. 'You mean, apart from him being the Son of God and you being a hairy fisherman? We-e-ll, you spend the night sleeping and Jesus spends the night praying. I guess that's one difference.'

Peter thumped the upturned boat he was sitting on. 'I do pray,' he declared, tugging his fist painfully out of the hole he'd made. 'At least,' he amended, sucking a splinter, 'I pray when it's stormy.

'Or when the mother-in-law gets one of her fits.

'At least, I try to pray.

'At least, I would pray if I knew how.

'OK, so I don't pray.'

James and Andrew were listening while they mended their nets. They put down the tangle of rope. 'I pray,' said Andrew, thoughtfully. 'But, oh, I dunno. I wouldn't say I know what I'm doing. Not really. Not like Jesus does.'

'He prays like I fish,' agreed James.

John nodded at a distant figure coming towards them. 'There he is, coming back now. 'Why don't we ask him how to pray?'

'Hang on,' said Peter, holding John back with a hairy hand the size of a paddle. 'What if he won't let me be his friend when he finds out I can't pray?'

John thought, *I should think Jesus knows that already.* But he didn't say anything.

Peter carried on: 'What if he says I have to stay up all night like him? What if he says I've got to talk in posh words? What if he says I've got to burble on like them Pharisees do? I can't be doing with that.'

'When did you ever hear Jesus talk in posh words, eh, Peter?' asked James.

'Yes, but… praying, James… that's not like talking…' But at that moment Jesus reached them and leaned comfortably along the sun-warmed wood of the boat.

'Ask him,' muttered John.

'No, you ask him,' muttered Peter.

'What's up?' asked Jesus. John stared at the birds circling overhead and whistled tunelessly. James and Andrew were suddenly very interested in the net again. Peter took a deep breath.

'Lord, you know John the Baptist taught his friends to pray…?'

'Yup?'

'Could you… would you…?' Peter looked at Jesus in desperation. 'Oh Lord, you know what I want, you always do. So why are you making me say it?'

'Go on, spit it out, Peter. I love it when you ask me for something.'

'Wewantyoutoteachustopray!' Peter blurted out.

Jesus grinned. 'Good start!'

James and Andrew dropped the net and looked at Jesus expectantly. John sat nearer.

'None of your religious stuff, though,' interrupted Peter, jumping to his feet and wagging a warning finger. 'Just something easy to remember—something we can say on the boat when the fish aren't biting, or first thing in the morning, or before we go to sleep. I do need a lot of sleep,' he added, before Jesus could bring in the all-night prayer idea.

Jesus nodded.

'And nothing too posh, either,' warned Peter. 'Or long. Or boring. Or…'

Jesus waited peacefully.

Peter stopped. And sat down again. 'Well, Jesus, you're the expert.'

'Pray like this…'. Jesus thought for a moment, then the words came out like jewels, each settling in just the right place to make a prayer as bright as a necklace.

'Father, help us to honour your name. Come and set up your kingdom. Give us each day the food we need. Forgive us our sins as we forgive everyone who has done wrong to us. And keep us from being tempted.'

Peter stared. 'Is that it? Even I can pray that.'

'It's a good start,' said Jesus. 'And talking of the food we need, I could really use some breakfast. Last one down the baker's is a wet sandal.'

Introduction

The Lord's Prayer has to be the ultimate in all-age worship—simple, straight from the Lord, easy to learn, full of down-to-earth requests with huge theological echoes; as valid if we take it at face value as when we try to wrap our minds round the massive kingdom vision that shines out in every phrase.

And it's all about relationships. It comes from Jesus and his friends talking together, and gives us a form of words to talk with our dear Father God together—because it is a 'together' prayer: '*Our* Father... give *us*...'. Adults and children, new Christians and old, Christians from all traditions, Christians down the centuries who are now with the Lord and those of us alive on earth today, we can all pray this prayer together with sincerity and integrity.

When we pray Jesus' prayer, we can look through Jesus' eyes for a moment. It gives us Jesus' snapshot of God the Father, the loving holy parent who longs to provide us with what we need, to help us in good times and bad and to work with us to bring his kingdom of justice, peace and love to every corner of the world.

It gives us Jesus' snapshot of the people he knows we can be—loving, grateful, living in a community of generosity, forgiveness and trust, working together with God and each other to bring about this kingdom of justice, peace and love.

Fewer and fewer schools are praying this prayer regularly. Fewer and fewer children are growing up knowing it by heart. We've got to pass this prayer on to the next generation. Some of them will pray it regularly and come to own it as it becomes part of who they are. Others may need it as a first aid kit, because when they feel lost and lonely in a dark world, or when their hearts are bursting with joy, they may need a form, a set of holy words rich with the resonance of goodness and wholeness, to express what this world gives them no words for. Just as soldiers in the World Wars prayed the Lord's Prayer as a default setting when they were too exhausted to find their own words, so we need to give our children this fall-back prayer for all seasons.

Interestingly, a good proportion of the children I ask about the prayer prefer the 'old-fashioned words' to the modern ones. Reasons given include 'I know it better', 'I like the words better', 'They're proper old words from the Bible from the old days', and 'It's got better punctuation'. I halted my enquiries at this point. As long as the language helps communication, let's face it, does it really matter which form is used?

This book aims to help children explore the Lord's Prayer and to own it for themselves. On the way, there may be times of fun, of noise and creative chaos, of quiet and stillness, of sights, sounds, smells and tastes as we meet with God through all our senses, our intellects and our hearts. We should be opening up as many questions as we answer, as the aim is to turn the prayer from a parroted meaningless series of words into a never-ending box of delights that grows as we grow.

It's written for KS2 children—the 7 to 11 age group—but will stretch happily either way a few years. There are oodles of different activities at different levels, so it could be used as a church group course or in school RE or assemblies. As the emphasis is on learning through fun, it would also be a good basis for a holiday club.

Using
The Lord's Prayer unplugged

The Lord's Prayer breaks up into ten phrases, so this book gives you ten sessions. In each session there are activities to help children explore what that phrase means. And rather than getting too theological about the inner meanings of the last word of the prayer, the final chapter not only looks briefly at what 'Amen' means but gives lots of suggestions for looking at the Lord's Prayer as a whole. You might want to glance at this session first so that you can use some of the ideas on the way.

In each session you'll find a variety of suggestions for ways of digging deeper into the Lord's Prayer.

There is a *Quiet space* in each session (see below for details). This could be a whole session in itself: it concentrates firmly on one phrase of the prayer and invites the children to spend time wondering about it in order to go deeper into it.

There are also plenty of suggestions for groups who prefer a more activity-based approach, with ideas for ice-breaker games, making Bible connections, praying, making and drawing.

As I am the ultimate in lazy leaders, I've tried to include plenty of ideas that take very little preparation and don't require you to assemble thousands of obscure ingredients each week.

Don't try to do everything in each session unless you are SuperTeacher of SuperGroup, and even then… You may not want to do an activity from every section every week: that's fine. A group may well enjoy simply doing the *Quiet space* wondering or just a craft, or maybe there will only be time for a prayer. Choose with care and prayer the ideas that suit your children and your space,

time and budget limits. Enjoy time to talk with and listen to the children in your group, rather than bombarding them with never-ending busyness. *No thunderbolts will fall if you don't get through the whole whack. Trust me on this.*

What's in each session?

Get your bearings

This part is for you, the leader/facilitator/teacher/ pressganged 'you need only do it for a week, honest' volunteer. It summarizes a little of what that week's section of the prayer is about and gives a bit of background.

Why not decorate your space…

Colour and visuals are important for all of us, especially children. You might want to set the scene by decorating your space in a different colour each session, and this section gives you some ideas of what to use. These colours are then picked up in the final chapter, in the *Godly Play* Lord's Prayer. Of course we won't be wallpapering the room a different colour every week, but it doesn't take long to throw in a few objects which help create an atmosphere and give children something to talk about. If you're from certain church traditions, it can also help to introduce the way liturgical colours are used in church. And it's fun.

Quiet space

You may want to use one or two of these questions just to open or close the session, but the *Quiet space* could be a whole session on its own, based on Jerome Berryman's *Godly Play* scheme. If you're using it as the whole session, set out art and craft materials and equipment in advance so that they are readily available to the children. You might like to put out a selection of coloured and white paper, card, paint, brushes, crayons, pencils, felt-tips, modelling clay, playdough and so on, with appropriate means of keeping surfaces clean—newspaper or plastic sheets, with wiping-up cloths at the ready.

Lay out some or all of the objects suggested on an attractive cloth or low table that helps the group to see them as 'set apart', and sit the group around the objects in a circle.

Spend some time with the group looking at the objects and talking about what is there. Then use the objects to open up the phrase of the Lord's Prayer by asking some of the wondering questions. Try not to impose your own ideas on the group, but listen actively to their insights. Welcome silence—a lot can be happening inside that doesn't surface in noise or talk.

After the wondering questions, ask the children what work they would like to do. Encourage them to use the art materials you have set out, in whatever way is right for them. Bring the group back together after their work time. This would be a good time to say the Lord's Prayer together, share something to eat or show what has been created.

Ice-breakers

These are games, activities, quizzes—enjoyable ways to set the scene and introduce the theme of the session.

Puppets

There's a short puppet sketch outline in each session which could be a good link through the weeks. There are no scripts to learn, just a 'plot' description. It picks up on a situation in which children might find themselves. Practise it beforehand with a glove puppet and a sympathetic audience (I find the dog is perfect), so that you can manage confidently without notes.

Bible exploring

The Lord's Prayer has echoes all through the Bible. In *Bible exploring* we pick up on the theme of the day both in the Lord's Prayer itself and in other stories or passages elsewhere in the Bible. There's a mixture of activities from challenging dramatic scripts for older children to act out to easy-to-understand storytelling suitable for any age.

Extra ideas

Little nuggets of activities for those fill-in moments, and interesting facts.

Prayer

Here you'll find different ways of praying on the theme of the session, again ranging from word-based prayers to action prayers, from shouting praise to stillness and reflection.

Songs

Some suggestions for songs on the theme. You should find them in books such as *Mission Praise* (MP), *Junior Praise* (JP), *Songs and Hymns of Fellowship* (SHF) and on CDs such as Kingsway's *Lovely Jubbly*.

Craft and art

Different levels of craft activity from the dead simple no-preparation-needed to the complex—but mostly dead simple.

Ongoing wall display

At the back of this book you'll find templates for each session, which you can photocopy, enlarge or simply cut out for the group to decorate to build up a wall display of the Lord's Prayer.

***

As you're trying to build up a whole picture of the Lord's Prayer, make time to pray it together every week. And try to recap on the work of previous weeks—reinforcement of stories, colours and symbols can only help.

So an hour's session might consist simply of *Quiet space*: wondering, individual response work, coming back together to say the Lord's Prayer and sharing something to eat. Or it might run something like: ice-breaker game, wondering questions, Bible story, prayer, craft.

I started this project rather unwillingly, as the Lord's Prayer always seemed a bit of a closed book—gabbled through too fast to make much sense of in church services, and too much part of those church services to think about praying it on my own. A friend, who is much holier than I am, told me once: 'I decided to pray the Lord's Prayer really slowly and think about what each bit means.'

'Oh yes?' I said.

'Yes. I started at the beginning, but an hour later I was still on "Our Father" so I haven't got to the end yet.'

After working on this book, I know what he meant. Plugs away… here we go…

1

Our Father in heaven

Jesus opens his famous prayer by telling us how to relate to God. 'Abba' is what a child would have called her father. 'Hello, Daddy' is the level of familiarity Jesus uses. Perhaps for adults 'Dear Father' gets across the implication of both intimacy and respect. Jesus invites us to chat to God in complete trust and openness, knowing that he's delighted to listen to whatever we have to say. He also asks us to say it together—'our Father...'. From the very start we are together with God and with each other.

These days, for too many children, the image of a father is an unhelpful one or even something completely foreign to their own experience. It is tempting to shy away from the image completely.

But should we assume that all the fathers Jesus knew in Nazareth were paragons of virtue? Did all the families in Nazareth have two parents? It's likely that Jesus knew what it was like to lose a dear father, as Joseph probably died before Jesus did. For those children who have what we might consider a good father figure, is even that person always a perfect role model? Of course not! All human parents inevitably fall short of God's perfect parenting. And shouldn't we be showing God the Father as the great parent that many children have been denied? For these reasons, and because Jesus wasn't afraid to tell us to call God 'Dad', we should explore the image sensitively but confidently.

The Bible has many more images that show God as a caring, nurturing source of life and security, including maternal images.

Why not decorate your space... GREEN?

Green is a colour of growth and life, which fits in with the idea of God as a parent who gives life to and brings up his children. Another image relating to nurture and guidance that Jesus uses to describe God is that of a shepherd—and green is the colour of grassy fields where sheep are safe and well fed.

You could roll out fake grass on the floor and use green balloons, cushions, pot plants, leafy branches or vases of flowers. Camouflage nets or football nets are often green and make an instantly effective backdrop.

Quiet space

Possible objects and pictures for focus:

- A variety of pictures of fathers, mothers, grandparents, prime carers
- A football
- A recipe book
- A shepherd and sheep
- A hen and chicks
- A baby
- Squares of coloured felt
- A light
- A globe
- A heart
- A cross

Lay out the objects and pictures for focus.

Say, 'Today we're thinking about the start of Jesus' special prayer—Our Father in heaven.'

Select some wondering questions from the list below. Ask the questions slowly and meaningfully, leaving space for reflection.

---

* I wonder which colour felt you would choose for 'Our Father in heaven'?
* I wonder which object or picture you would choose to go with 'Our Father in heaven'?
* I wonder what picture is in your mind when you pray this part of the Lord's Prayer?

---

* I wonder what words you choose to start your prayers with?
* I wonder why Jesus put this into the Lord's Prayer?
* I wonder if it reminds you of any people Jesus met?
* I wonder how God feels when we call him 'Father'?
* I wonder which object or picture he would choose to go with us?
* I wonder if we could leave out this part of the Lord's Prayer and still have all the prayer we need?
* I wonder what you like best about this part of the Lord's Prayer?
* I wonder how you would pray this part of the Lord's Prayer with just your hands?

Spend a moment thinking about how we talk to God our Father in our hearts, or out loud, or with our hands.

Take the square(s) of felt that the children have chosen and the pictures or objects they chose and place them on display for the rest of the session.

Either choose from the activities below or give the group the opportunity to do their own work to explore this part of the prayer based on the wondering questions. Supply art and craft materials if you choose the second option.

Ice-breakers

Father Abraham

 Sing the action song 'Father Abraham has many sons' as an energetic warm-up. The words of the verse are:

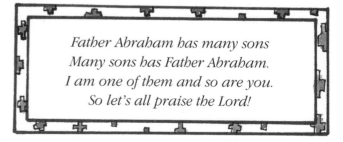

Father Abraham has many sons
Many sons has Father Abraham.
I am one of them and so are you.
So let's all praise the Lord!

Then, at the end of each verse, everyone calls out one of the phrases in the order below and, during the next verse, waves, swings or shakes that limb. The actions are added on verse by verse until everyone is waving both arms, both legs, nodding their head, and turning around: the final 'sit down' comes as something of a relief!

Right arm / Left arm / Right leg / Left leg / Nod your head / Turn around / SIT DOWN!

As everyone collapses, say that today you're thinking about the idea of all Christians having one father—that we're a family together with not only Abraham as our great-great-great-great- (and so on) grandfather, but also with God as our great father in heaven.

(If the girls complain that they're not sons but daughters, you can either say that 'daughters' doesn't scan, or you could explain that in Abraham's time it was the sons who inherited everything from their father and, in that way, we're all more like sons than daughters. Or you could say, 'Glad you noticed. Let's sing "daughters" every other verse.')

Names

You'll need a family tree or a multi-generation photograph of your family.

Talk about the people in the photo or family tree and what relationship they all have to each other. For example, I'm married to Paul. My children are Arthur and Judith. My parents are Les and Jen. Jen's parents are Eric and Mary.

Then ask what these people might call each other. For example, what would I call Les? What would Judith call Paul? What would Arthur call me? What would Jen call Eric? Suggest very formal names like 'Papa' until the children agree that you would call your father something like Dad or Daddy.

Say that Jesus says we can call God, our heavenly father, just the same thing that we call our dads.

Puppets

You will need a glove puppet.

Have a chat with your glove puppet. The gist of the situation is that you tell the children you're very upset because your puppet is hiding, won't speak to you, won't even look at you. You (with the children's help) manage to persuade him to tell you what the matter is: he's scared of talking to you as he's found out you're such an important person because… (find a reason why you might be important—your job, your role in the church, the fact that you're a grown-up, so big…) He's worried he might have to make an appointment to see you, or fill in a form, or that you won't think he's worth bothering with.

You reassure the puppet (with the children's help) that you really want him to chat to you, because you love him very much. You love spending time with him—just like God loves us to spend time chatting to him, as Jesus tells us in the start of the

Father Abraham

Composer: Unknown

Lord's Prayer. He even tells us to call God 'Daddy'!

Your puppet ends up happily chatting in your ear, snuggled up to you.

Passages about *Our Father in heaven*

- The prodigal son (Luke 15:11–32)
  Jesus' story shows how loving and forgiving God our Father is, whatever we do.

- Jesus' teaching on prayer (Matthew 7:7–12)
  We think about what it means to ask a loving parent for what we need, not a machine or a committee.

- One family (Ephesians 3:14–15)
  Paul writes about the whole Christian family being joined together under God the Father, and we think about the character of that heavenly father.

The prodigal son

LUKE 15:11–32

As we wonder what sort of a father God is, we can look at Jesus' story of the prodigal (meaning 'recklessly wasteful') son. You could ask the group to decide, as they hear the story, whether it is more about the son or the father.

The version below is clearly based on Jesus' original, but as you tell it, the group needs to fill in the details for you to make it their own version: these opportunities are shown in the text in bold.

***

Everybody loved Super Sausage! Super Sausage was the lovable cartoon hero of a whole range of books, TV programmes, computer games… **Anything else?**

There was all sorts of Super Sausage merchandise. There were Super Sausage lunchboxes, Super Sausage duvet covers, Super Sausage pencil cases… **What else was there?** All in all, the Super Sausage empire was making lots and lots of money.

Now the man behind Super Sausage was not only the richest man in the world, but he was also the kindest, nicest, most generous person you could ever meet. Think of the nicest person you know… **Who is it?** Well, if it's possible, this man was even nicer than that! He loved Super Sausage, he loved his

work, but more than anything he loved his two children, Sam and Sidney. He used to show them round the factory and say, 'One day, my sons, all this will be yours.'

Both boys worked for their dad. But the boys were very different from each other. Sam was a very hardworking lad… **What time do you think he got to work in the morning?** That's right! **And did he stop for a coffee break? A lunch break? A tea break?** That's right! **And what time did he work till at night?** Yes, you're right—Sam worked really, really hard.

But Sidney was a different kettle of fish. Sidney was a complete slob… **What time did Sidney get up in the morning?** Yup. **And how long was his coffee break? His lunch break?**

His tea break? And do you think he worked right up to the time he was supposed to? That's right—he hardly did any work at all!

One day, Sidney was even more fed up than usual… **What was he doing in his office?** OK, well, he stopped doing that and he got up and he climbed the stairs up to his dad's office and he said, 'Dad! I'm fed up! Gimme my share of the factory now. I want to go off and enjoy myself for once.'

How do you think his dad felt? What might he have said? Well, what he actually said was, 'Here you are, Sidney, take your share of the business.'

How do you think Sidney showed how happy he was? Yes, after he'd done all those things, he ran down the road, dashed into a bank, sold his shares, realized he was a multi-millionaire and went on a shopping spree… **What did he buy?**

And with all these things in his brand new suitcases, he flew in his new helicopter to the Big City and booked himself into the best hotel… **whose name was …**

Then he ran down to the bar and shouted to all the people there, 'Hey everybody! The drinks are on me!' And suddenly he found he had hundreds of new friends! Sidney wanted to show them how much he liked them being his friends… **so what do you think he did for them?**

They had a marvellous time for weeks doing all these exciting things. But then one day, Sidney said to his friends, 'Um, can anyone lend me a fiver? I've run out of money.' **And did his friends help him out?** Absolutely not! **What did they say to him?** And they all left him.

Poor Sidney was all alone with no money and he had to sell all the lovely things he'd bought, to pay his bills. And he had nothing to eat! He had to find a job quickly to earn some money.

But because he'd been such a slob at school, he couldn't find any job except a really horrible dirty smelly one… **What do you think it was? What sort of things did he find to eat? What was the worst thing about it?**

Well, while he was doing this terrible job, suddenly he came to his senses. 'What am I doing here?' he said to himself. 'Back at my dad's factory, no one has to do such a terrible job.' **And what did he decide to do?** Yes, he decided to go home to his dad. **Was he happy to be going home? Was he worried by anything?** Yes—he said to himself, 'What is my dad going to do to me when he finds out I've wasted all that money?'

Meanwhile, back at the factory, Sam and Sidney's dad was anxiously looking out of his window across the city, as he did every day, to see if his son was coming home at last. And then he saw Sidney! **How do you think he felt?**

He ran down the stairs and belted down the roads across the city until he got to his son… **Did he tell Sidney off for wasting all that money?** No, he felt so sorry for him, he flung his arms round him and gave him a big cuddle.

'Oh Dad, I'm sorry,' said Sidney. 'I've been so bad. I'm not good enough to be your son.'

And did his dad agree? No! He shouted to his workers to fetch some clean clothes (Sidney was still a bit niffy) and told them to get some food ready for a party to celebrate Sidney's return… **What sort of food did they cook?**

When big brother Sam realized what was going on, was he pleased to see his brother again? No, he was furious. He stomped up to his dad and he grumbled, 'Dad, I've worked all this time and you've never even given me a bag of crisps! And this slob comes home after wasting all your money and you throw this big party for him! It's not fair!'

'Dear Sam,' said his dad. 'You're always with me and everything I have is yours. But we had to party because your brother was lost and now he's found! Hip hip hooray!'

✳ ✳ ✳

You could use some or all of these questions:

- What words would you use to describe the dad in this story?
- Can you think of a time when you were surprised because you thought you'd get told off and you got a cuddle instead?
- Why did Jesus tell this story?

There is a text message version of the parable to decode in *The Gospels unplugged*, also published by BRF, which older children may enjoy.

Jesus' teaching on prayer

MATTHEW 7:7–12

In the Lord's Prayer we see Jesus telling us to call God 'our dear Father' or 'Daddy'. We also see the idea of a parental relationship in Jesus' other teaching on prayer. Jesus shows his listeners how unthinkable it would be for a human dad to play jokes on his children or put them in danger when they ask him for what they need—so how much more ridiculous it is to think that God, our perfect heavenly Father, might treat his children so badly!

In this silly sketch, we introduce the idea that we are in a relationship with God, not a formal mechanical set-up.

The children may like to read and perform the script. Then you could suggest that they make up their own scene—they could use the same idea of somebody trying to get something that they need, and having to do all sorts of ridiculous things to get it. (Perhaps they need help with homework or a drink of water, or something from a high shelf.)

Talk about how silly that would be when all you have to do is ask the person who looks after you to help.

After the sketch, you could look at Matthew 7:7–12 together. Remind the children that Jesus is speaking these words to his friends and crowds of people who had come to listen to him on a mountainside.

You could ask the children to put the passage in their own words.

Is God more like a slot machine or a parent? Why?

I need my tea!

Characters: Joe and Izzy
Props: pen and paper, table and chair

Izzy is sitting writing at the table.

JOE:	What are you doing?
IZZY:	I'm filling in this form.
JOE:	What for?
IZZY:	'Cos that's what I have to do.
JOE:	What do you mean?
IZZY:	Look, I'm hungry!
JOE:	So…?
IZZY:	So I need to fill in a form.
JOE:	Why?
IZZY:	To get my tea!
JOE:	Why do you have to fill in a form to get your tea?
IZZY:	'Cos that's the way it works, dumbo! I fill in the form, then I go and wait in the queue to get it stamped.
JOE:	But…
IZZY:	Then when it's stamped, a secretary takes it to the committee…
JOE:	Really?
IZZY:	And if the committee aren't in the mood, they all shout 'NO! GO AWAY!' into a loudspeaker. It's very embarrassing.
JOE:	Um. Yes, it would be.

 Reproduced with permission from *The Lord's Prayer Unplugged* published by BRF 2004 (978 1 84101 262 9)

IZZY:	But if the committee agree that the form's OK, the secretary brings it back.
JOE:	And…?
IZZY:	And I put it in that machine and I press the button…
JOE:	Yeah?
IZZY:	And if I've done it wrong, a custard pie flies out and hits me in the face.
JOE:	Oh dear.
IZZY:	But if it's all filled in just right, the machine prints out a little slip of paper…
JOE:	Mmm?
IZZY:	And I take the little slip of paper and I go to the other machine and I feed it into the machine and I wait and the other machine whirrs a bit…
JOE:	And?
IZZY:	Well, if something's gone wrong or if the engineer's in a bad mood, sometimes it gives you a plate of cowpat.

JOE:	Oh dear.
IZZY:	But if you're lucky, and if I've filled in the form right and I haven't done anything wrong, and the engineer's feeling happy, and if he's not too busy and if everything's working as it should…
JOE:	Yes?

IZZY:	Then I get my tea, of course!
JOE:	Oh. It seems a bit… well, difficult.
IZZY:	What do you do when you're hungry, then?
JOE:	I just ask my dad…
IZZY:	And ….?
JOE:	And he gives me my tea.
IZZY:	What? Just like that?
JOE:	Yeah. He's my dad!

One family

EPHESIANS 3:14–15

For this reason I kneel before the Father, from whom his whole family in heaven and on earth derives its name. (NIV)

Say that when Jesus starts his prayer by calling God 'Dear Dad', he's saying something very important about how we can see God.

All of us have somebody who looks after us. We all know what it's like to be cared for. But Jesus says that God is our Father in heaven—he is like our parents when our parents are at their very, very best! Peter Graves, in his book *Living and Praying the Lord's Prayer* (BRF, 2002), quotes six-year-old Michael, who, when asked why we call God our father, replied, 'Because when your dad's his very goodest, he's just a little bit like God.'

We're going to imagine now what the very best parent ever might be like.

You'll need large pieces of paper—for example, wallpaper backing roll, pencils, coloured pens.

This activity is done in pairs, named A and B.

Ask the pairs to imagine the Best Parent Ever. A lies down on the floor, on top of the paper, and B 'sculpts' them—puts A's body in the position called 'The Best Parent Ever'.

Now B draws round A in pencil so that there is an outline of a person on the paper when A gets up. Label this outline 'Best Parent Ever'. Roughly where the heart is, draw a heart shape.

The pairs could then do some or all of these activities together.

- Go over the outline in colour. What colour or colours will you use for Best Parent Ever?
- What expression would you draw on their face?
- What pattern would you draw on their hands?
- If you could draw one object to give them, what would it be?

- Round the outside of the Best Parent Ever, draw what sort of things that parent might do (for example, give enormous presents, play football with me…). You might like to introduce the idea here that you're not thinking about your best friend, but about a parent—might there be some things you would need a parent to do that a best friend wouldn't do? (For example, telling you off when you do something wrong.)
- Inside the outline, draw pictures of things to show what the parent is like. (For example, if you think the Best Parent Ever is strong, you might draw a tank or a mountain; if you think they're gentle, you might draw a butterfly.)
- Draw a speech bubble coming from their mouth. In it, write something they might say.
- Draw a thought bubble coming from their head. In it, write or draw something they might be thinking.
- In the heart shape, write or draw what you think is dearest to them—what or who they love best in the world.

Display all the outlines around your meeting room. Give the group some time to go round and look at them all. Then, if it is appropriate, you might like to ask the pairs to talk about their pictures, explain difficult parts of them or say what they like about other pairs' ideas.

Say 'If Jesus asks us to call God "our Father in heaven", what do you think God our Father is like?'

Extra ideas

The good shepherd

JOHN 10:11–18; PSALM 23; LUKE 15:3–7

 The shepherd of the flock is a picture that is closely related to the idea of God as father to his people. The children could act out the story of the lost sheep, or improvise a scene showing the difference between the good shepherd and the hired hand. There is a rap version in *The Gospels unplugged*.

God our mother

PSALM 17:8; ISAIAH 66:13; HOSEA 11:1–4

All the above passages are interesting examples of God's love described in very maternal terms.

Happy families

After playing the card game, you could hold up one of the completed families at the end of the game, and ask what the children of that family would call their father. If the group suggest 'Dad' or 'Daddy', get them to laugh by challenging them and saying things like, 'Would they really? Are you sure? Wouldn't they call him "Sir" or "Your Lordship" or "Magnificent One"?'

Other silly ideas for formal names are 'Sire', 'Oh Esteemed Ancestor', 'He Who Must Be Obeyed', and silly abusive or casual ones might be 'Oy you', 'Slave', 'Whatsyername', 'Fatface'. Keep challenging your group to say why the children would call him Daddy or Dad, until everyone has got the idea that your suggestions are either terribly formal or terribly rude. The children call their father 'Daddy' because they want to show him that they're very close to him and also that they want to please him, not be rude to him.

Say that today you're looking at what Jesus tells us we should call God when we pray to him.

Father says...

Play 'Simon Says', but instead of the commands being obeyed only when you start the command with 'Simon says', they should be obeyed only if you begin them with 'Mum says', 'Dad says', or any other names for parents (Mama, Papa, Mumsy, Pops, Daddikins—they can be as silly as you like). You might like to ask the group at the end what difference it makes to call someone 'Father' or 'Daddy'. Jesus broke new ground in prayer by calling God 'Abba'—Aramaic for 'daddy'—instead of the very formal 'father'.

Prayer

Response prayer

 Here is a prayer to say together, a leader (perhaps an older child) saying the line and all joining in on the response.

LEADER:	Please join in with the words 'Thank you for your love'. Our father in heaven:
ALL:	Thank you for your love.
LEADER:	You're the strongest, kindest dad we could ever imagine.
ALL:	Thank you for your love
LEADER:	You give us our life.
ALL:	Thank you for your love.
LEADER:	You give us families at home and at church.
ALL:	Thank you for your love.
LEADER:	You give us arms to hug with.
ALL:	Thank you for your love.
LEADER:	You show us the right way to live.
ALL:	Thank you for your love.
LEADER:	You love us even when we make you sad.
ALL:	Thank you for your love.
LEADER:	You love us more than we can possibly imagine.
ALL:	Thank you for your love.
LEADER:	Our Father in heaven
ALL:	Thank you for your love. Amen

Picture prayer

You'll need backing paper, double-sided sticky tape, and pictures from magazines showing people caring for someone else (or for something else)—pictures of parents holding children's hands, school crossing patrols, farmer with animals, child with a pet, children hugging, nurses and patients and so on.

Put all the pictures out on the floor or table and ask the children to look through them, then to choose the one that most reminds them of the way God looks after us. Put some double-sided tape on the back of the pictures they choose.

As they stick their chosen picture on to the backing paper one by one, they might like to explain why they chose it. You could ask if it reminds them of any stories in the Bible that they've heard.

Finish with a prayer along the lines of: 'Dear

heavenly Dad, we love you so much for being... (use the words the children have used as they talked about their pictures). Help us to remember that whatever we do and however old we get, you will always love us just as much as you do now.'

Story prayer

Remind the children of the parable of the lost son (Luke 15:11–32). Ask them to imagine that they are the son who has come home to his dad, and it's the moment in the story when the dad gives him a big hug and welcomes him back home. Imagine the father turning to smile at you and asking, 'What did you miss most about being with me?' Ask the children what they would say. Turn any suitable answers into a prayer, thanking God for these wonderful things that we enjoy about being with him.

Songs about God as our Father

Father God, I wonder (MP 128)
Father in heaven (SHF 712)
Abba Father (MP3)
My God is so big (JP 169)
Father, I place into your hands (MP 133)
Father, we adore you (MP 140)
He's got the whole world (JP 78)
Lovely jubbly (Kingsway CD, Doug Horley)

Craft and art

Church family tree

You'll need the outline of the family tree photocopied from the template on page 113, and pens.

Using the outline, children can fill in and decorate a 'Christian family tree', with God as the father of us all. They can fill the spaces with people in the church family who are special to them.

Three-dimensional tree

You'll need a branch; a flowerpot and soil; card leaf outlines; hole punch; gold string; felt tips.

Again, picking up on the idea of a family tree, the group (or individuals) could secure a large branch in a plant pot and draw members of the church family on to individual leaf-shaped cards. Punch a hole in the cards and thread gold string through the hole, then hang them from the 'family tree'. You could write a sign to attach to the 'trunk' saying 'God is our Father'.

T-shirt decorating

You'll need plain T-shirts, fabric pens or paints and an iron and ironing board (if the pens need ironing to fix them).

Get the children to think of a positive word they can put in the gap: 'You think I'm......? I take after my dad.' (Or 'I take after my mum.') Suggestions are cool, strong, tough, gorgeous, brilliant, cuddly, a super-hero, a mega star. They can write their sentences on their T-shirts in fabric pen, perhaps half on the front (You think I'm cool?) and half on the back (I take after my dad). And of course they can add appropriate decoration. The activity reinforces the idea of having the same traits as our parents, just as Christians grow more like God.

Ongoing wall display

The picture today is of a parent hugging a child. You will find the template on page 123.

Hallowed be your name

Get your bearings

Jesus tells his friends they're praying to a very holy God. Hallowed… holy… sacred… set apart… precious… special: God is our dad, but he's also mega-holy.

We've seen that he's as near and dear to us as our own family, but now we're reminded that he's also more holy than we can begin to imagine. Jesus reminds us to keep both sides of our relationship with God in balance.

Before we ask him for anything, before we thank him for anything, before we think of other people or ourselves, we think about who God is. We put him in first place.

Holiness is something that may be alien to a society as informal and matey as ours. Jesus asks us to reclaim that sense of holiness—the awe and wonder of God. We concentrate on what it means to honour him in the way we live lives of praise and worship. For children, this may mean taking prayer time seriously, standing up for God in a godless playground, or refusing to use God's name as a swear word.

It is very hard for us to grasp the significance of names in biblical times compared with now, without going into a great deal of detail. For the sake of understanding, we take 'your name' to mean 'your character, your reputation, you yourself'.

In today's session, we look at God's holiness through the biblical symbols of light and fire.

Why not decorate your space… BLACK?

Black can be mysterious and 'otherly'. It can represent the darkness into which God shines the fire and light of his holy presence.

Black fabric or dustbin bags cut open or fringed create a dramatic effect. (To avoid suffocation, don't allow children to play with dustbin bags.) If you can do it safely, you could have candles burning in the darkness to illustrate the flame theme. Or you could cut flames from yellow or red cellophane. (Positioned near a fan, they can give an interesting flame-like effect.)

Quiet space

Possible objects and pictures for focus:

* Names of the group written individually on cards
* Names of God on cards (see 'Extra ideas' in this session)
* A book of babies' names
* A candle
* Incense
* Pictures of God as a powerful holy God
* A very fragile ornament
* Squares of coloured felt
* A globe
* A heart
* A cross
* A light

Say, 'Last time we thought about "Our Father in heaven". Today we're thinking about "Hallowed be your name".' Lay out the objects and select some questions from the list below.

> ✳ I wonder what 'hallowed' means?
> ✳ I wonder which colour felt you would choose for 'Hallowed be your name'?
> ✳ I wonder which object or picture you would choose to go with 'Hallowed be your name'?
> ✳ I wonder what picture is in your mind when you pray this part of the Lord's Prayer?
> ✳ I wonder why Jesus put this into the Lord's Prayer?
> ✳ I wonder if it reminds you of any stories?
> ✳ I wonder how God feels when we remember that his name is holy or hallowed?
> ✳ I wonder which object or picture he would choose to go with us?

> ✳ I wonder if we could leave out this part of the Lord's Prayer and still have all the prayer we need?
> ✳ I wonder what you like best about this part of the Lord's Prayer?
> ✳ I wonder how you would pray this part of the Lord's Prayer with just your hands?

Spend a moment thinking quietly about how holy God is.

Take the square(s) of felt that the children have chosen and the pictures or objects they chose and place them on display for the rest of the session.

Either choose from the activities below or give the group the opportunity to do their own work to explore this part of the prayer, based on the wondering questions. Supply the art materials if you choose the second option.

Ice-breakers

Hallowed!

 This is suitable for older children. Make a story circle—sit everyone round in a circle. The space inside the circle is the acting space. If one of the group wants to come and start acting out the story you tell, they can put up a hand. If you choose them, they come and start acting as you speak. If you want to clear the space, you wave your arms over the space and everyone in it sits back down in the circle, so that someone new can come and act.

Tell one or more of the following stories, giving opportunities for members of the group to come and act them out. The endings aren't given: at the point where the story stops, ask the actors to carry on acting to a suitable end.

Footballing Frank

 Frank was running along the pavement, dribbling his football. He was going really fast and didn't see a pothole in the pavement. He tripped up, kicking the ball as he fell.

When he got up, he looked for his ball, but

it had vanished. He peered all down the street, but there was no sign of it. He shrugged and was just about to give up when he caught sight of it. There it was, behind a wire fence. Frank shook the fence but it was very strong. Then he saw a sign on it. There was a picture of a figure being zapped by a bolt of lightning. He read the words 'Danger of Death! 12,000 volts. Keep out! Southern Electricity'. His ball was lying there, just behind a sort of terminal with wires coming out of it. Frank scratched his head. What should he do?

Footballing Fatima

 Fatima threw herself down in her chair. She was really fed up. Her brother had nicked her football and lost it and Sue was coming round any minute for a game. There was a knock at the door. Yes! There was Sue in her shorts and football boots, all ready for a game. Fatima let her in. She told Sue what the problem was. Sue smiled from ear to ear. 'Don't worry!' she said. She picked up the brand new top-of-the-range X-Box that Fatima had got for her birthday. 'We can kick this about instead!'

What would Fatima say?

Footballing Fred

 Fred was furious! He stood in the middle of the football pitch and jumped up and down in his fury. 'It's not fair!' he shouted. 'That ref doesn't know what he's doing! He's useless!' To his surprise, the rest of the team came and stood behind him. Joe nodded. 'We agree!' he yelled. 'And to prove it, we're not going to take any more notice of you, Ref!' The rest of the players nodded. 'Yeah! That's right! We're not going to listen to you!'

Joe drop-kicked the ball across the pitch and the game began again…

Write up on a flipchart or similar the names from the three stories—Frank, whose ball went into a dangerous 'keep out' area; Fatima, whose friend suggested they use the X-Box as a football; and Fred, who played by his own rules, ignoring the referee.

Ask these questions and write up the answers:

- In each story, what/who could you say was 'hallowed' or set apart?
  (The fenced-off area; the X-Box; the referee.)

- Why had those things or people been set apart?
  (The area was dangerous; the X-box was valuable; the referee needed to be outside the action to judge it fairly.)

- What happened when they stopped being set apart?
  (Frank's life was in danger; the X-Box was wasted and was no good for its proper purpose; the game of football was ruined.)

Then, looking at those answers, ask why the group thinks Jesus prayed that God's name would be hallowed or set apart?

Power!

This activity shows how dangerous it can be to mess about with powerful things.

Write the following on slips of paper:

- Look into the sun
- Eat a really HOT vindaloo curry
- Let off an extra-loud-banging firework next to your ear
- Put your finger in a candle flame
- Stand in a shed full of cows with diarrhoea, no doors or windows and no clothes peg for your nose
- Put a large block of ice down your neck
- Drink a cup of boiling hot coffee
- Eat a lemon
- Put your earphones on for your Walkman without realizing the volume's turned to maximum
- Sniff your brother's smelly sock
- Look into a car's headlights when they're on full beam

Put the slips of paper into a box.

Ask the children to take it in turns to pull a slip out of the box, read it to themselves, then act out what would happen if they tried to do what it says. For example, if they tried to look at the sun, they might mime being dazzled. The rest of the group try to guess what has happened to them and why.

Point out that some pretty ordinary things are so powerful that we should treat them with respect. When Jesus says in his prayer 'Hallowed be your name', he's helping us to understand that God himself is not just our dear old dad, but someone incredibly powerful—and we should treat God with respect!

Puppets

You will need a glove puppet.

 The situation is that your puppet is upset: some children in the school playground have been making fun of a girl in his class because she goes to church. He doesn't know what to do. You find out that, for the puppet, it feels as if these children have been making fun of God as well, and that makes him very sad.

You explain to him that he's upset because he wants God's name to be hallowed. Of course the puppet doesn't understand this word. Can any of

the group explain what it means? Agree with the group that it means 'holy' or 'special'. Say that when people don't know how lovely God is, sometimes they make fun of him, or use his name as a swear word, and this is upsetting.

Ask the group what the puppet could do in the playground. Agree on a good suggestion and reassure the puppet that Jesus wants God's name to be special and hallowed too, like he says in his prayer.

Bible exploring

Passages about *Hallowed be your name*

- The burning bush (Exodus 3)
  Moses meets God, recognizes his holiness and learns his name.

- In God's name (Colossians 3:17)
  Paul tells the Colossian Christians to do everything in God's name—to be ambassadors for him. This drama activity looks at what an ambassador might have to do.

- Hallowed be your name
  A verse script to explain what the word 'hallowed' means.

The burning bush

EXODUS 3—4

This is a quiet, meditative version of the story. You might like to get your group lying down with eyes closed to listen so that they can see it in their imagination. Or you might want to use some simple models to 'act out' the story—Moses, a sheep and a goat, a bush—that can be moved about as the action dictates.

Introduce the story by asking what 'hallowed' means (holy, sacred, set apart, special). Say that the very first time in the Bible that the word 'holy' appears is the time when God tells Moses what his name is. Ask them to listen in the story for the ways God shows his holiness.

***

 Picture the countryside—far out in the wilderness. Towering mountains, rough red dusty ground, green patches of scrubby grass and wild herbs for the sheep and goats to graze on. Low twisted trees in bleached browns and olive green, and knee-high bushes whose branches graze your legs as you stride through them. No one around for miles: an empty still place where the bleating of the flocks echoes from rock, to rock, to rock. You can pick out the different voices of the flock. You know each sheep and goat by name and they know you, their shepherd.

Only one bird sings. Heat rises from the baked ground, even this early in the day, through the soles of your sandals. You need to keep an eye open for water in a place like this, somewhere you've never explored before.

As you scan the countryside for a stream, something catches your eye in the stillness—a flicker of movement, a glimmer of light.

You're a shepherd: you've got all the time in the world to find out what it is.

You pick your way towards it. As you get nearer, you frown in puzzlement; you can see quite clearly what it is—a little low bush like the ones you've been walking through all morning. But this one is in a clearing on its own and it's on fire… but as you watch, it doesn't burn up—it just stands with the gold and green and blue flames flickering along its branches. 'Strange,' you think. 'I've seen a lot of odd things in Egypt and in Midian, but I've never seen that before. Trick of the sunshine in my eyes? I'll go over and see why it's not burning up.'

The sheep and goats are strangely silent as you turn your back on them and clamber through the undergrowth towards the burning bush, leaning on your shepherd's stick. You can see more clearly as you get nearer. The flames are only hand-sized at most, but each one is charged with energy, as if a volcano or a forest fire had been squeezed down and compressed, to burn controlled within each flame. The tension is unbearable. It could explode at any minute. The bird has stopped singing. And in the hot, clear quiet you hear a voice…

'Moses!'

If someone calls you by name, if someone knows you out here in the empty wilderness, what can you say? The obvious, of course…

'Here I am.'

The voice is coming from the burning bush.

'Don't come any closer. Take off your sandals—the ground where you are standing is holy.'

This is so weird; it's no time to argue. You take a step back, just in case. Who or what is talking?

And the voice continues…

'I am the God who was worshipped by your ancestors, Abraham, Isaac and Jacob.'

Definitely no time to argue. Vague memories of stories about this God, so different from the smart-alec Egyptian gods, stir in your memory—a God of flood and fire, a God made by nobody, but who is himself the maker of the world.

Without taking your eyes off the bush, you slip the sandals off your feet and feel the soft hot dust under your soles and the stab of tiny shards of gravel. You feel very unprotected without your sandals on. There is nothing between you and the fire.

God speaks. You listen.

'I have seen how my people are suffering in

Egypt. I have heard them beg for help. I feel sorry for them. I will bring them out of Egypt into a country where there is good land. Now go to the king of Egypt. I am sending you to lead my people out of his country.'

You? A shepherd? A nobody? Rescue God's people out of Egypt?!

'Who am I that I should do that?'

'I will be with you.'

A million panicky questions rise up. You say, 'I'll tell the people of Israel that the God of their ancestors has sent me to them. But what should I say if they ask me your name?'

The flames on the branches leap upwards and flare out over the whole sky. The world is on fire. Those flames could swallow you up and turn you to dust in a second. The words echo out, unforgettable…

'I am the God who was and is and will be for ever. So tell them that "I am who I am" has sent you. That is my name.'

The flames are drawn back into the burning bush. God—'I am who I am'—tells you what you are to do, gives you power to do it, gives you secret words that burn in your heart and light the way ahead.

Then the flames melt and vanish upwards into the shimmering air.

The bird sings. The sheep bleat. The bush is just a bush. And you are just a barefoot shepherd—a shepherd with a bigger job than you had before.

***

Ask the children to tell you the story of what happened in their own words.

Why might Moses know that he was in the presence of a holy God?

What does 'holy' mean?

What might a god be like who wasn't holy?

In God's name

COLOSSIANS 3:17

Whatever you say or do should be done in the name of the Lord Jesus, as you give thanks to God the Father because of him.

This is an activity for older children.

If we pray 'Hallowed be your name', we are praying that we can be part of that process. So what is it like to live and act 'in the name of' somebody?

Ask the group who knows what an ambassador is. (Perhaps you know a real ambassador who could come and talk to the group about their work.)

This sketch shows a king giving power and authority to an ambassador to speak and act in the name of the king.

When you've read it through, the children may like to divide into groups and act out Helen in Jellibeania, trying to deal with one or more of the different situations suggested at the end of the sketch.

Ask the groups before they start: Will she manage it on her own? Will she need to ring up the king to ask his advice? How will she make sure the people respect the king's name in the way she deals with them?

KING: Ah! Helen! Splendid!
HELEN: You sent for me, your Majesty?
KING: Yes indeed! Got a job for you, as it happens. Like to take it on, eh?
HELEN: I swore allegiance to you, your Majesty, and you can ask me to do anything you like.

KING: Excellent! I need an ambassador
           in the region of Jellibeania and
           you're just the chap to do it!
HELEN: Um, what's an ambassador, your
           Highness?
KING: I can't be everywhere at once,
           can I? As an ambassador, you'd
           be my representative in
           Jellibeania. Stand in for me, if
           you like. Be my eyes and ears
           and hands over there.
HELEN: But... I'm only a poor subject of
           your kingdom! How can I
           possibly stand in for you?

KING: Oh, you know me well enough
           to know what I think about
           most things that come up. Just
           imagine you're me and ask
           yourself what I'd do.
HELEN: But you're so much better at
           ruling than I would be! What if I
           make mistakes?
KING: You're bound to make mistakes!
           But I know you'll always want
           my royal name to be respected,
           so if you keep that in mind, you
           can't go far wrong. And I'm on
           the end of the phone whenever
           you want to chat things through.
HELEN: But I'm not a king!
KING: No, but I'm giving you the
           power and the right to act in my
           name. The authority, if you like.

What you say counts as what I
would say. If you sign your name
to anything, that's the same as
me signing my name there. If
you do something, it's as if I
were doing it.
HELEN: Your Majesty! What an honour!
KING: Yes it is, isn't it? Now listen—the
           situation in Jellibeania is this:
           (a) There are some isolated
           villages in Jellibeania who have
           never heard of the king. They
           have no idea of the good things
           the king wants to give them
           (drains, electricity, education,
           improved health care, liquorice
           allsorts).
           (b) There are two families at war
           in Jellibeania. The Bloggs are
           saying that ten years ago the
           Smiths stole a bag of jelly babies
           off them. They've been at
           daggers drawn ever since and
           many family members have
           been killed. The king is very
           fond of both families and
           doesn't want anyone else to
           suffer in this silly conflict.
           (c) The chewing gum factories
           of Jellibeania are polluting the
           rivers with toxic overflow.
           (d) There is a harsh boss of a
           chocolate factory in Jellibeania
           who is making her labourers
           work so hard, they have no time
           to give to their families.

Watch the finished scenes and ask: 'What do you
think the people of Jellibeania would think of the
king after Helen had dealt with their problem?'

Hallowed be your name

Of all the lines in the Lord's Prayer, this is the one
most likely to be misheard and misunderstood by
children, because of the archaic word 'hallowed'.
Here is a short scripted two-voice poem that explores some of the misunderstandings. Children
could read this through in pairs

1 Hallo God! Hallowed be your name.
  Is that the same as 'hallo God'?

2 No, not quite the same.

1 Well is it hollow God?
  Hollow like a log?

2 No, it's not the same at all.
  It's not holl- but hall-
  Hallowed be your name.

1 Hallowed be your name. OK.
  Does it mean his name's 'Hallowed'
  Like Bob or George or Jack
  Or Ron or Sid or Harold?

2 No. How can I make this clear to you?
  Hallowed is something dear to you,
  Holy, precious, set apart,
  Sacred, special, closest to your heart,
  Something you hold on to,
  come what may,
  Something you rule your life by,
  night and day,
  Something with power: all untouchable,
  Something beyond you: all unreachable.

1 So 'hallowed be your name' means more
  than just a prayer—
  It's how I live my life every when,
  everywhere?

2 Your prayer is just the start. Make it your
  aim
  To live your life in every way to hallow his
  name.

***

You could follow up the sketch with this matching
activity. Photocopy the following statements and
Bible verses on to card or paper, cut them up, mix
them up and ask the children to pair them up.

What do these bits from the Bible tell you about
God's name? Match up the verse with what it tells
us about God's name. Younger children may need
the whole verse printed out. Older ones may get
more out of looking up the verses in the Bible.

God wants us to keep his name special.

*You shall not misuse the name of the Lord
your God. (Exodus 20:7, NIV)*

If you know God's name, you can rely on him
when things get tough.

*Those who know your name will trust in you.
(Psalm 9:10, NIV)*

God's name has got more power than a whole
army!

*Some trust in chariots and some in horses,
but we trust in the name of the Lord our God.
(Psalm 20:7, NIV)*

If we really want God's name to be hallowed,
it might mean doing something difficult.

Jesus said just before he talked about how he
was going to die, *'Father, glorify your name!'
Then a voice came from heaven, 'I have
glorified it and will glorify it again!' (John
12:28, NIV)*

God's names

 Did you know that our name 'God' is
written in loads of different ways
through the Bible? Here are some of the
Hebrew names for him and what they mean:

El:	God (Deuteronomy 5:9)
Elyon:	Most High God (Genesis 14:19–20)
Yahweh (or Jehovah):	'I am who I am' or 'I will be what I will be' or 'I will do what I will do' (Genesis 12:8)
Adonai:	My Lord—used instead of reading aloud 'Yahweh', because Yahweh is such a holy name
El Olam:	Everlasting God (Genesis 21:33)
Yahweh-nissi:	The Lord is my banner (Exodus 17:15)

Yahweh-jireh:	The Lord provides (Genesis 22:14)
Yahweh-shalom:	The Lord is peace (Judges 6:24)
Yahweh sebaot:	The Lord of the armies of heaven and earth (1 Samuel 1:3)
Attiq-yomin:	Aramaic for Ancient of Days (Daniel 7:9)

Race through a Gospel each in four teams and find out what different names people call Jesus.

Jesus says 'I am…' (like an echo of God calling himself 'I am who I am' or Yahweh) and gives himself different names, especially in John's Gospel. What 'I am' names can you think of?

- the bread of life (John 6:35)
- the light of the world (John 8:12)
- the gate (John 10:9)
- the good shepherd (John 10:14)
- the resurrection (John 11:25)
- the way (John 14:6)
- the true vine (John 15:1)

Power = Danger

Pretend you're going to put your hand in a candle flame. Give it a big build-up, but when the children protest, ask why you shouldn't. Agree that it's really stupid to mess about with something that's as powerful as fire. Perhaps you'll put the candle somewhere safe, apart from the group. This will tie in with the idea that Jesus is reminding us to respect God and to keep him sacred, or set apart. (You might want to throw in the 'Don't try this at home' warning.)

Hallowe'en

Hallowe'en is short for 'the day before All Hallows', or All Saints' Day, which is the day when we remember Christian people who have died and are with Jesus. All Saints' Day is on 1 November.

The highest name

Read Philippians 2:6–11.

Ask the children to go off in small groups and choose one reader per group. The rest of the group add some actions to the reading to show what it means. They might like to make it into a stylized dance or mime. They could spend some time practising, then come back together and, if they like, show the others what they have produced.

Prayer

Barefoot prayer

 Ask the children to take off their socks and shoes. Ask how it feels to have nothing on their feet. If possible, take them for a short walk somewhere where they can feel different textures underfoot.

Ask when they take their shoes off—perhaps when they go into a house, so that they don't spoil the carpet. Say that in biblical times, and in some religions today, taking your shoes off is a mark of respect. It could also be the sign that you were a slave.

Remember that God told Moses to take off his sandals as he was standing on holy ground. Say that it's good to remember that the God we worship is not just a dear father, but a really holy God, whom we should respect. Say that we can show this respect in many ways, and one is in how we pray. Say that you're going to say one prayer sitting, one kneeling and one standing. (You might like to practise moving from one position to another without fuss and noise.)

Sit in a circle with legs out in front of you so that all the bare feet are visible, and pray:

Dear God, our feet are bare and unprotected. We come before you, knowing that you are an incredibly holy God. Thank you that you use your great power to protect us.

Then kneel in the circle and say:

Dear God, our feet are bare, like slaves' feet were bare. We kneel before you as your servants. Help us always to keep your name holy.

Then stand in the circle and say:

Dear God, our feet are bare as we stand before you. Help us to remember how holy you are in all parts of our lives.

Hallowed be your name

Light a candle in the middle of your circle to represent God's holiness, like the burning bush.

Ask the children to think of all the different areas of their lives and of the world around them where they would like to see God made number one, or hallowed. You might like to talk briefly about the sort of ways this might happen.

Make a list of the situations, big and small, on a big sheet of paper, and then pray a simple response prayer. For example:

LEADER: Dear Father, in my school…
ALL: Hallowed be your name.
LEADER: In my football club…
ALL: Hallowed be your name.

Number one prayers

You'll need lots of number ones photocopied from the template on page 114 and cut out of paper or card.

Ask the children to think of what they will do tomorrow. You might need to talk them through

the routine—getting up, going to school, lessons, playtime, lunch, going home, clubs, TV, tea, bedtime and so on. As they imagine each stage of tomorrow, ask them to pick up a number one if they would like God's name to be hallowed—if they would like him to be number one at that time of the day. At different points, you might ask how that might happen. How can God be number one in the playground, for example?

Finish by saying 'thank you' to God that he wants to be in every part of our lives.

The children could stick the number ones to a sheet of backing paper with 'Hallowed be your name' in the middle, or take them home to remind them the next day who is number one.

Extra ideas

 Organize a bonfire party or campfire party so that children living in centrally heated houses and flats have a chance to experience the power of fire as an element. Obviously there is the safety aspect to consider, so do make sure that you have adequate supervision and have put safety precautions in place.

Songs about God's name

Jesus, name above all names (MP 375)
The greatest thing in all my life (MP 646)
Ascribe greatness (MP 40)
You are mighty (SHF 1125)
El-Shaddai (MP 119)
Jehovah Jireh (MP 354)

Craft and art

Footprints

You'll need pens, trays of different coloured paints, large sheets of paper, and some old flip-flops, espadrilles, plimsolls or sandals—also newspaper and cloths to clear up the mess!

This is a really messy activity!

The idea is to make a picture of the story of the burning bush.

The children should draw a burning bush on the paper, then show what Moses did by making his footprints—first in sandals as he walked up to the bush, then barefoot as he listened to God, then however the children think he might have gone away. Barefoot? In sandals? Running? Skipping? Crawling?

Suggest that the children make the different footprints by walking in the paint and on the paper.

What's in a name?

You'll need photocopies, Bibles or story Bibles and felt tips/crayons.

Photocopy the chunky word GOD from the template on page 114 and give a copy to each child. Ask them to think of all the stories they can that show what power there is in God's name—for example, creating the world, feeding the five thousand, coming back from the dead. Ask them to draw inside the letters of the name GOD cartoons that show scenes from these stories, so that someone looking at the finished picture could see what power there is in God's name.

Number one

You'll need different construction/craft materials.

You could do this activity in a variety of different ways to suit your group and your resources. Basically the idea is to make a 'number one' to show that when we pray 'Hallowed be your name', we want God to be number one in our world and in our lives. You could challenge the children to make the biggest, the most attractive, the most exciting, or a number one that shows something about God. Here are some suggestions.

- Use loads of Lego, Meccano, K'nex or a similar construction toy to make a number one.
- Junk modelling—have lots of boxes, packets, and so on available, plus sticky tape and glue. Ask the group to make a number one either individually or as a group.
- Provide the outline of a number one on card, photocopied from the template on page 114, and ask the group to decorate it with pens/stickers, or write on it 'Hallowed be your name'.
- Use air-drying clay in different colours from which to make a number one badge.
- Use quilling to fill in the outline of a number one. This could be symbolic of the tense power there is coiled up in the name of God.

Ongoing wall display

Today's picture is of the burning bush.
You will find the template on page 123.

3

Your kingdom come

Get your bearings

We've established whom we're praying to—our dear, loving, heavenly father. We've reminded ourselves how holy this father is and put him in number one place in our prayer. Now Jesus tells us to pray big: we're to match our hearts to God's heart and to pray for his heavenly kingdom to be established on earth. Oof. This sounds an enormous prayer.

But when we look at the parables that Jesus tells about God's kingdom, they are very reassuring. Jesus talks about little things like yeast and mustard seeds. He talks to little people like Zacchaeus and is delighted when they come into the kingdom. The kingdom that Jesus has come to bring is one that starts with a baby... with a few buckets of water... with a packed lunch... By the grace of God, these small beginnings explode into a man who changes history, a party with enough wine to open an off-licence, five thousand people stuffed full of food.

So while the prayer 'Your kingdom come' is a huge prayer in one sense, we can pray it with integrity and faith because it is based in small everyday situations. Wherever love triumphs, God's kingdom comes, whether that's at the dramatic hacking down of the Berlin Wall or when a sister manages not to thump her brother in a dispute over the last piece of chocolate cake. God's kingdom comes each time love overrides selfishness. And it grows and blossoms and gives fruit of love, joy, peace, patience...

So in today's session we look at what Jesus says about God's kingdom and how we might expect to see his kingdom coming.

Why not decorate your space... ORANGE?

Orange is bright and cheerful and has a fruity connection. You could have a bowl of fruit—oranges, satsumas, peaches, apricots. Orange cellophane over a light source gives a lovely warm glow. (Make sure it's not too near the light source or you may have more of a conflagration. If in doubt, get some proper lighting gels from theatrical suppliers.) Balloons, of course, are always good.

Quiet space

Possible objects and pictures for focus:

- A crown
- A crown of thorns
- Pictures of kings and rulers from around the world
- Pictures of children from around the world
- A church
- Squares of coloured felt
- A globe
- A heart
- A cross
- A light

Say, 'We've thought about "Our Father in heaven, hallowed be your name". Today we're thinking about "Your kingdom come".'

> ✱ I wonder which colour felt you would choose for 'Your kingdom come'?
> ✱ I wonder which object or picture you would choose to go with 'Your kingdom come'?
> ✱ I wonder what picture is in your mind when you pray this part of the Lord's Prayer?
> ✱ I wonder why Jesus put this into the Lord's Prayer?
> ✱ I wonder if it reminds you of any stories?
> ✱ I wonder how God feels when we ask him to let his kingdom come?
> ✱ I wonder which object or picture he would choose to go with us?

> ✱ I wonder if we could leave out this part of the Lord's Prayer and still have all the prayer we need?
> ✱ I wonder what you like best about this part of the Lord's Prayer?
> ✱ I wonder how you would pray this part of the Lord's Prayer with just your hands?

Spend a moment asking God to build his kingdom somewhere that's special to each member of your group.

Take the square(s) of felt that the children have chosen and the pictures or objects they chose and place them on display for the rest of the session.

Either choose from the activities below or give the group the opportunity to do their own work to explore this part of the prayer based on the wondering questions. Supply the art materials if you choose the second option.

Ice-breakers

Fruit salad

 Sit the children in a circle on chairs or cushions. Give each child a name of a fruit—apple, orange, banana, plum—round the circle. Then choose one person to go in the middle of the circle, and take away their seat.

Call out one of the fruits, and all the children with that name have to swap places. The person in the middle tries to sit in one of the empty seats so that you end up with a different person in the middle. If you call 'Fruit salad', everyone has to swap places. This can be played for ages without boredom setting in.

Use the game to introduce the idea that God's kingdom is like good fruit—it's a place where God supplies good things for his people; where God's people make good things happen, not bad things; and where their lives are full of goodness and love.

Good king, bad king

This game is based on 1 Samuel 8.

Ask who's in charge of a kingdom. It's a king or

queen, of course. Say that when the people of Israel wanted a king, the prophet Samuel told them they would be much better off trusting God to be their king. Samuel warned them of all the terrible things a king would do to them.

Here are some things a king or queen might do. If you think each thing is something a *good* king might do, run to one end of the room. If it's something a *bad* king might do, run to the other end.

Call out the following, not in this order:

- He'll drag you off to war.
- He'll make you work in his palace for free.
- He'll charge you high taxes.
- He'll live in a palace with jacuzzis and yachts and widescreen TVs while his people starve.
- He'll make you slaves.
- He'll take your house if he feels like building a summerhouse there.
- He won't have time to listen to little people.
- He'll protect you from your enemies.
- He'll make sure there are good laws in the country.
- He'll make sure the poor people have enough to eat.
- He'll look after you when you're not well.
- He'll teach people who want to learn.
- He'll make the country a happy place to live.

- He'll always find time to listen to his people.
- He'll organize parties and invite everyone along.

Finish by asking, 'I wonder who is the best king ever? I wonder what sort of things he does that are like our list of "good king" actions?' Help the children to think of times Jesus looked after people when they were unwell, listened to people and so on, and then talk about people and governments who do these things today.

Say that if we want God's kingdom to come, we need to behave like Jesus the king.

Puppets

You will need a glove puppet.

 The scene today is that your puppet is very sad. He's hiding under a newspaper. When you coax him out, he shows you the sad stories in the paper. He's been watching *Newsround* and there are lots of terrible things happening in the world. You can tell him that it is sad when wars and disasters happen. But he can help! By praying for God's kingdom to come, he can change little things in his own life and big things like whole countries. You can send him away with the newspaper to start praying for all those sad things.

Bible exploring

Passages about *Your kingdom come*

- Don't worry (Matthew 6:25–34)
  Jesus talks about the contrast between the stressful life of those outside his kingdom and the peace and trust that God promises inside his kingdom.

- Kingdom parable (Matthew 13:31–32)
  Jesus tells one of many stories to show what God's kingdom is like.

- Perfect kingdom (Revelation 21)
  A vision of God's perfect kingdom in Revelation.

Don't worry

'Don't worry' is a rap to act.

A is running round and round in circles, getting faster and faster with each verse. B walks forward with a jaunty step on the beat, in a straight line. A and B could be played by groups speaking together or individuals.

A Gotta get going, gotta beat the rest
Gotta own the most, gotta be the best.
B Gonna work for God, gonna give him me
Gonna be the girl [boy] he wants me to be.
A Gotta eat the best food, gotta wear the best kit,
Gotta get the best marks, gotta go for it.
B Gonna put my life in my Father's hands
Gonna do what he wants, you understand?
A Gotta go faster, gotta beat the rest,
Gotta have much more, gotta be the best.
B Gonna trust, gonna ask for what I need
Gonna build his kingdom in word and deed.
A Gotta grab, gotta chase, gotta steal, gotta cheat,
Got no time to listen, I might get beat.
B Gonna shout out loud: Your will be done!
My life's gonna say: Your kingdom come!

A And me, I say: My will be done!
Gotta run… gotta run… gotta run… gotta run…

A collapses exhausted in a heap. B freezes mid-walk.

You could ask the children:

* What do you think people worry about?
* Do you think they need to worry about these things?
* Does God want us to worry?
* How can we stop worrying?
* How much worry do you think there is in God's kingdom?

Kingdom parable

The kingdom of heaven is like what happens when a farmer plants a mustard seed in a field. Although it is the smallest of all seeds, it grows larger than any garden plant and becomes a tree. Birds even come and nest on its branches.

> *You'll need a picture of a tree with birds nesting in its branches, photocopied from the template on page 115.*

Talk about things that start off small and end up enormous. The children will have lots of their own ideas but here are some examples to get you going: seeds, *Harry Potter* books, babies, raindrops, chains of shops like Boots that started off with just one store, bacteria and so on.

Ask the children to get into pairs or groups, to choose one of the ideas and make up a 30-second TV advert for this wonderful thing that starts off so small and ends up so large.

After admiring, and possibly videoing, their adverts, read out the short parable of the mustard seed from Matthew 13:31–32. Show the picture of the tree. Jesus says that the kingdom of God is like this mustard seed. Ask the children:

* What do you think this story is really about?
* What sort of tiny things might start off God's kingdom?

- Why do you think God likes to start off with tiny things?
- What might this parable have to do with your life?

You might like to point out that Jesus told lots of other parables to help us understand different things about God's kingdom. (Look at the rest of Matthew 13 for a start.)

Perfect kingdom

> *You'll need brochures/pictures of theme parks like Disneyland, and other pictures of beautiful places or houses, palaces and so on, drawing tools, Lego, playdough and similar construction/modelling materials.*

Show the pictures of the 'perfect places'. Talk about what is good about them (for example, beauty, order, fun, excitement) and what might be bad (for example, queues in Disneyland, poisonous spiders on desert islands, exclusiveness of entry because of price).

Ask the children to imagine for a minute that they have all the money they need to design and build a really absolutely perfect kingdom. Ask them to imagine what it might look like, what the people might look like (if it had people), what sort of mood there would be in that kingdom, what would make it exciting and fun for everyone to be in, who would be in charge.

Ask the children to choose which materials they would like to work with, and to make or draw that perfect kingdom with those materials.

When everyone's finished, compare the results. Perhaps choose the things that everyone agrees are best out of all the ideas, to make the ultimate kingdom. Then say that right at the end of the Bible, in the book of Revelation, John, the writer of the book, gets a glimpse of God's perfect kingdom.

Read Revelation 21:1, 3–4:

I saw a new heaven and a new earth. The first heaven and the first earth had disappeared, and so had the sea… I heard a loud voice shout from the throne:

God's home is now with his people. He will live with them, and they will be his own. Yes, God will make his home among his people. He will wipe all tears from their eyes, and there will be no more death, suffering, crying, or pain. These things of the past are gone for ever.

Ask some of the following questions:

* I wonder what you like best about this kingdom?
* I wonder what it's like to live in a home with God?
* I wonder what it's like to live in a place where no one is ever sad?
* I wonder if this world is ever like the new earth?
* I wonder what there will be in the new kingdom that will be even more fun and exciting than the things you've imagined for your perfect kingdoms?

Extra ideas

A true story about two kingdoms

 Tell the children this true story.

✳✳✳

 Sometimes you can see a kingdom of this world trying to shut out the kingdom of God. There was once a Christian pastor in Romania, called Richard

Wurmbrand. The government in Romania wanted to stop all Christianity in that country, so Richard and his wife were put in prison simply because they were Christians. They had a son who was nine years old. When they put his parents in prison, the government sent this boy away to school. This school was one that taught how good the government's ideas were, and how silly it was to believe in Jesus. All through the rest of his school life, the boy was kept at this school, while his parents were kept in prison.

Years passed like this, and the boy grew up into a young man. At last, after all those years of being told how useless Christianity was, he was allowed to go and see his mother in prison. She was overjoyed at the thought of seeing her son again, but also very worried. 'It will hurt so much if he makes fun of Jesus,' she thought. 'But he has been in the power of these people for so long. All I can do is trust God.' And she prayed for him in love, as she had done every day of his life.

The day came for the two of them to meet, and the mother braced herself to hear her son make fun of the faith that had kept her in prison all those years. But when her son arrived, he looked at her face and saw the marks of suffering and the joy of her spirit. And he said to her, 'Mother, if Christ means this much to you, then I want him too.'

This little light

You'll need a copy of the NASA picture of electric lights all over the earth, taken from space. It can be ordered from PO Box 37, Bognor Regis, PO21 1AJ or viewed at http://antwrp.gsfc.nasa.gov/apod/ap001127.html.

Say that sometimes it can seem useless to do our little bit for God's kingdom. What effect can our tiny actions possibly have?

Show the children the picture of lights: each individual light is tiny but altogether they make a huge difference to darkness.

Spend a moment in quiet, asking God to help you build his kingdom on earth.

Prayer

Heart prayer

You'll need a heart made of wood, felt or similar.

 Sit in a circle and pass the heart round the circle. As each person takes it, they can pray either out loud or in their own heart for God's love to come into the life of someone they know.

Drawing prayer

You'll need a large sheet of paper, and pens.

Draw a big heart on a large sheet of paper. Ask everybody to think in silence for a moment of the people and places they would like to feel God's love. Invite them to write or draw those people and places inside the big heart. When they have finished, draw a big cross over the whole heart and pray, 'Thank you, Lord, that you love these people and places with all your heart.'

Little seed prayers

You'll need mustard/cress seeds, yoghurt pots, paper towels, water.

As you scatter the seeds on the damp paper towels in the yoghurt pots, you could pray out loud that God's kingdom will grow in each child's life, starting in the tiniest ways and becoming bigger than we can possibly imagine.

Songs about God's kingdom

 Seek ye first the kingdom of God (MP 590)
All over the world (MP 18)
Go, tell it on the mountain (MP 179)
This little light of mine (JP 256)
Jesus' love is very wonderful (JP 139)

He's got the whole world (JP 78)
Peace is flowing like a river (MP 554)
The Lord is a great and mighty king (MP 655)

Craft and art

Kingdom cards

You'll need A4 card, scissors, felt-tip pens (optional), heart stampers, world map or stencils of countries and people.

1. Fold the A4 card in half widthways.
2. Open it out again and, on one half of the card, draw or stencil the outline of a country shape or a person that you'd like to be filled with God's love.

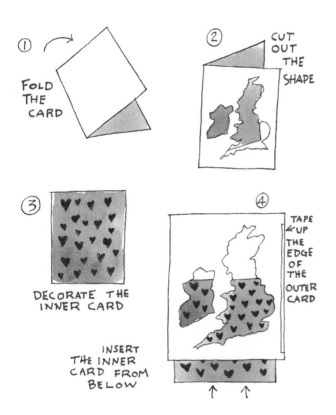

① FOLD THE CARD

② CUT OUT THE SHAPE

③ DECORATE THE INNER CARD

④ TAPE UP THE EDGE OF THE OUTER CARD

INSERT THE INNER CARD FROM BELOW

3. Cut out the shape from the centre of the card. Younger children may need adult help to avoid cutting through the edge. Tape the long edges of the folded card together, but leave the top and bottom ends open.
4. Take a second piece of card, just under A5 size (half A4), that will fit inside the previously folded card. Either colour the small card in, or decorate it with hearts all over.

5. You should be able to slide the small card into the end opening of the larger one, and see the person or country gradually 'fill up' with God's love as the colours enter the cut-out shape.

Hearts

You'll need lots of hearts cut out of all shapes and sizes and types of paper in different shades of red and pink, glue, and backing paper.

Invite the children to make a collage showing God's love, using the hearts.

When they have designed their collages, invite them to explain why they have pictured God's love like that. Give lots of praise and encouragement.

Big challenge

You'll need sheets of newspaper, scissors, sticky tape.

Challenge each group or pair to make their single sheet of newspaper seem as large as possible. They can cut, fold and stick it as much as they like.

What starts off small can become surprisingly large!

Ongoing wall display

Today's symbol is a crown of thorns.
You will find the template on page 124.

4

Your will be done on earth as in heaven

Get your bearings

This phrase is tied in closely with the previous one—'Your kingdom come'—and one phrase seems to give the answer to the other. How will your kingdom come? By people doing your will. But hang on, *we're* praying this prayer—and that brings us face to face with the question of whether we're prepared to do God's will, not just rely on some godly nerve gas being sprayed on the land which will take away our will and brainwash the world into doing what God wants.

Doing God's will is an act of *our* will. Jesus invites us to pray that our actions and the way we live our lives will be in the best interest of others, rather than self-motivated. Then life on earth will become as eternal, joyful, deep-down good and

fair as we'll find it is in heaven. If everyone did what God wanted, we would surely have heaven on earth. That's not going to happen yet, but hey, what if *we* do what God wants?

Just as we saw that the kingdom of God begins in tiny ways, here we see that seeking God's will begins not with huge multi-national powerhouses, but with the smallest decisions in our own lives. We're working from the starting point that God wants us to 'love the Lord our God with all our heart, soul, mind and strength and love our neighbour as ourselves'. In other words, we put God and other people first.

Jesus knows that it isn't always easy to do God's will. In this session we look at his own heartbreaking struggle in Gethsemane to submit to what his Father wanted, although it meant letting go of the life he loved on earth.

Why not decorate your space... RED?

Why red? Red is traditionally the colour of God's love, of passion. It also reminds us of the blood of sacrifice.

Decorate the space to be as red as possible, with hearts and crosses. As well as red cushions, rugs or posters, you could use union jacks, which have not only red but also three crosses to talk about. Red balloons, especially helium-filled foil heart-shaped balloons, are great.

Quiet space

Possible objects and pictures for focus:

- A Christmas list starting 'I want...'
- People smiling/enjoying being together/helping each other
- A gate
- A church
- A number one
- A globe
- A heart
- A cross
- A light

Say, 'We've thought about "Our Father in heaven, hallowed be your name. Your kingdom come". Today we're thinking about "Your will be done on earth as in heaven".'

✳ I wonder what we're praying for when we say 'Your will be done'?

✳ I wonder which colour felt you would choose for 'Your will be done'?

✳ I wonder which object or picture you would choose to go with 'Your will be done'?

✳ I wonder what picture is in your mind when you pray this part of the Lord's Prayer?

✳ I wonder how different heaven is from earth?

✳ I wonder why Jesus put this into the Lord's Prayer?

✳ I wonder if it reminds you of any stories?

✳ I wonder how God feels when we ask him to let his will be done?

✳ I wonder which object or picture he would choose to go with us?

✳ I wonder if we could leave out this part of the Lord's Prayer and still have all the prayer we need?

✳ I wonder what you like best about this part of the Lord's Prayer?

✳ I wonder how you would pray this part of the Lord's Prayer with just your hands?

Spend a moment asking God to let his will be done in the life of someone you know.

Take the square(s) of felt that the children have chosen and the pictures or objects they chose and place them on display for the rest of the session.

Either choose from the activities below or give the group the opportunity to do their own work to explore this part of the prayer, based on the wondering questions. Supply art and craft materials if you choose the second option.

Ice-breakers

Quiz: Who comes first?

You'll need signs showing A, B or C.

 Put the signs in different parts of the room. Call out the question and the possible answers and ask the children to run to the letter that goes with the answer they'd give.

1. **If there's only one piece of yummy sticky chewy chocolate cake left, do you...**

   a) Say, 'Here, little brother. You can eat it'?
   b) Grab it and stuff it in your mouth before anyone else can?
   c) Cut it up and share it with the rest of the family?

2. **You've got 50p pocket money. You quite fancy a king-size Mars bar. Then you see the charity shop poster which says that people are starving in another country. Do you...**

a) Say, 'Oh dear' and go and buy your Mars bar?

b) Buy a snack-size Mars bar and give the rest to the charity shop?

c) Give the whole 50p to the charity shop—you weren't that hungry anyway?

3. **Your leader says it's time to say a prayer. Do you…**

a) Try hard to listen to God and talk to him?

b) Close your eyes and think of nothing at all?

c) Groan and grumble and mutter so that no one else can pray either?

4. **There's someone in your class you really don't like, but they're on their own at play-time. Do you…**

a) Think, ha ha, serves them right?

b) Ask them if they'd like to join in your game?

c) Not take any notice of them?

5. **Your leader asks you to spare a Saturday afternoon to do a sponsored walk in aid of church funds. Do you…**

a) Collect as many sponsors as you can?

b) Turn up but not bother collecting much money?

c) Not bother with it—the money's not for you, after all?

Sit everyone down and run through the questions again, this time asking first what good would come from doing the 'right thing', then asking what they would have to give up each time if they were going to do the 'right thing'. Point out that putting what God wants first, or putting other people first, often involves giving up something valuable. It might not always be easy, but it can make a big difference to the world around us.

Mighty Master game

You'll need a chair.

'Your will' and the subjunctive 'be done' aren't expressions that we use in everyday speech. It's worth making sure that everyone understands the basic meaning of the English, before you start on the theology.

Take it in turns to be the Mighty Master in this game. When you are the Mighty Master, you sit in the chair that is your throne. You can issue a command and everyone else must do your bidding. So the Mighty Master says, *'It is my will that you…* all clap your hands!' Everyone replies, *'Your will be done, oh Mighty Master'* and everyone claps their hands. The next Mighty Master sits in the chair and issues his or her next command with the same phrase: *'It is my will that you…* (jump up and down, scratch your armpits, sing Humpty Dumpty and so on)'. Continue until everyone has had a turn.

Ask what it means to say, 'Your will be done'.

Puppets

You will need a glove puppet.

 Today the puppet is making a big scene about being sick. He keeps ducking behind the stage to throw up. You make enquiries and find out that he's just eaten an enormous bag of sweets all by himself. You ask, what might have been a better idea? It would have been good to share them round, wouldn't it? He shamefacedly brings out a second bag that he'd been planning to eat—but this time he wants to share it with everyone. That makes him very happy and he stops feeling sick.

You could remind your puppet that God's way of sharing and giving to other people, rather than being selfish, is always the best way.

Bible exploring

Passages relating to the theme of *Your will be done*

 • Jesus' choice (Luke 22:39–46)
Jesus prays in the garden of Gethsemane that God's will, not his own, will be done.

- Adam and Eve disobey God (Genesis 3)
  Adam and Eve choose to do what they want, not what God wants.

- David (Psalm 40:1–11)
  David declares how much he wants to do what God wants, and also describes what it's like to try to wriggle out of doing it!

Jesus' choice

This passage explores what happened to Jesus in the garden of Gethsemane as he prayed, 'Not my will, but yours, be done.' Sometimes we may think it was easy for Jesus to do what God wanted all the time, but maybe it was just as difficult for him as it is for us.

In the monologue below, Peter, one of Jesus' closest friends, relates what happened on the night we now know as Maundy Thursday. Ask the children to sit or lie comfortably and close their eyes so that they can imagine the scene. The monologue is based on the account in Matthew 26:36–46, Luke 22:39–46 or Mark 14:32–42.

***

 It was night time by the time we'd finished supper. We stumbled after Jesus as he strode off into the dark. Through the sleeping streets of the city and up the hill, the flap, flap of his sandals on the stones getting further and further ahead. Good job we'd been this way with him each night that week—I don't think we'd have found him otherwise. We caught up with him under the olive trees at the top. It was one of his favourite places, that garden. Ancient olive trees creaking and rustling in the night's quiet. Deep rich smell of earth and bark. Peaceful up here. A hideaway to pray in. Not that Jesus looked peaceful, though.

'Pray that you won't be put to the test,' he muttered, and walked off while we glanced at each other—you could just about pick out liquid eyes and white teeth in the spare moonlight. Then one by one we sat down on the warm earth.

Jesus blundered a little way away through the trees, but then he dropped to his knees. Didn't mean to listen in, but you could hardly help it, the way he called out like his heart was breaking: 'Dear Father, if it's what you want, please don't make me suffer by making me drink from this cup…'

'What cup?' I thought, through the waves of sleepiness that threatened to overcome me. Supper was over now. Nobody was going to poison his wine, were they? But the pain in his voice made me realize it wasn't a normal cup he was on about. John, beside me, was muttering some lines from Isaiah the prophet: '…the cup filled with the Lord's anger…' I wondered drowsily what a drink like that would look like… smell like… taste like…

It came to me that this was the first time I'd ever heard Jesus unwilling to do what God his father wanted him to. Odd, that. But he hadn't finished.

Jesus was still praying, but the words inched out as if they were animals being dragged to the altar, digging their hooves into the ground and straining away from the knife. His teeth were gritted: 'But do what you want, and not what I want.'

I wanted to run away from the feeling of storm clouds gathering around us. I remembered we were supposed to be praying. I sat up and peered over at Jesus—he was bent double, as if he'd got stomach ache or cramp. His fists were clenched. He was all curled in on himself, a tight ball of misery, like there was a battle going on inside him. Then I thought he must have been stabbed in the dark—because I heard these thuds of what sounded like big drops of blood splatting on the ground. I jumped up to help, but I saw someone was there already, wiping his forehead, putting his arm around him. And Jesus wasn't bleeding at all. It was sweat dripping off him. I sank back down. Those storm clouds. Must remember to pray.

Next thing I know, there he is shaking us all awake. 'Why are you asleep?' he demanded. Something had changed while we'd been asleep. Now he was calm, as if he'd made up his mind about something. 'Wake up and pray that you won't be put to the test.'

I was just about to pray, just getting round to it.

But at that moment we heard the marching.

* * *

You might like to ask the children some of these questions:

- What was Peter feeling when he was in the garden with Jesus?
- What was Jesus feeling?
- What surprises you about this story?
- Has there ever been a time when you've found it really hard to do what God wants instead of what you want?

Adam and Eve disobey God

Right at the beginning of the Bible we read the story of Adam and Eve choosing to do what they want instead of what God wants. Below is a script to perform or read, based on Genesis 3. With older children, you could help them compare what happened in the garden of Eden and the garden of Gethsemane.

Characters: God, Adam, Eve, Serpent

GOD: Yo, Adam, Eve, the world is yours! It's dead exciting, innit? It's excellent, most excellent. So relish every minute.
There's just one thing—you see that tree? The one with all the fruit?
You eat from that and you'll be dead, so please, my dears, don't do it.
There's loads of other things to eat, there's fruit and veg galore; So stick to those and you'll enjoy this place for evermore.

ADAM: Hey Eve, dig these bananas! They're scrummy, squishy, sweet.
I never knew that there could be so many things to eat.
I love this lettuce. Try these turnips. Taste this big tomato! But keep clear of the gherkins— they make you want to—

EVE: Start to
Be polite, please, Adam. You're right, though, this is yummy.
It's very kind of God to give all this to fill my tummy.

Reproduced with permission from *The Lord's Prayer Unplugged* published by BRF 2004 (978 1 84101 262 9)

SERPENT:	But just a minute, sweetie. Just wait a teeny mo. Are you sure that God said that this tree here was no-go? He simply wants you to stay thick. He told you both a lie. You eat this fruit, you'll be like God. Of course you won't just die.
EVE:	Oh are you sure? He was quite firm. The one thing he said no to.
ADAM:	Hey Eve! Try this! I think I've found the very first potato!
SERPENT:	A clever girl like you should see it can't do any harm To nibble just one tiny bite. Go on—reach up your arm…
EVE:	The tree is very beautiful…
ADAM:	Hey Eve! I've found a pea!
EVE:	Its fruit looks good…
SERPENT:	It is! It is! Go on, my sweet, trust me!
EVE:	I've got the right to be as wise as God himself, no doubt.
SERPENT:	You're right! You're right! Just pick the thing!
ADAM:	You've got to try this sprout!
EVE:	There! I've got one! Just one bite! Mmm, that is really wicked. Hey Adam, try this fruit—it's fresh—it's one that I've just picked.
ADAM:	Isn't it from off that tree God said we shouldn't touch?
EVE:	Oh it's all right, I just picked one. I haven't taken much.
ADAM:	Well, if you're sure. Here goes. Oo-er. I think my brain is popping. Something tells me now we've started, there's no way of stopping.
GOD:	Adam? Eve? Where are you? You're hiding? What? From me?
ADAM:	We can't come out! You'd make us blush! We've nothing on, you see.
GOD:	Who told you you had nothing on? Who cared, right up to now?

	You've eaten fruit from off that tree! How could you do it? How?
ADAM:	It wasn't me, sir, it was Eve. It's all her fault, not mine.
EVE:	Oh no, it was the snake, not me, he tricked me…
GOD:	Please don't whine. Right, snake, eat dirt.

SERPENT:	Oh hiss, oh hiss. Well, I'm not finished yet.
GOD:	And Adam, Eve, your perfect lives will fill with pain and sweat. By choosing your own way, not mine, one day you'll have to die. And you must leave my garden now. Goodbye, my dears, goodbye.

You could ask the children:

- What did Adam and Eve enjoy most about their perfect world?
- Why did Eve choose to do the one thing God told her not to do?
- How did Eve feel when she realized she had made the wrong choice?
- How did Adam feel?
- How did God feel?

David

You'll need Bibles, paper, drawing materials.

The first part of Psalm 40 is about finding help when it's tough, but also about David wanting to do what God wants.

 Reproduced with permission from *The Lord's Prayer Unplugged* published by BRF 2004 (978 1 84101 262 9)

Read Psalm 40:1–11 together. Spend a moment to think about the words. Jesus would have known this psalm by heart.

- What do you think was in Jesus' mind when he was praying in the garden just before his arrest?
- What do you think helped him, according to the psalm?
- Does the psalm help us understand what he was thinking?

King David wrote this psalm—it's the song of a king. Let's explore it for a bit.

I patiently waited, Lord, for you to hear my prayer. You listened and pulled me from a lonely pit full of mud and mire.

- What do you think it feels like to be stuck in a deep hole?
- Do you think the king was in a real pit?
- What do you think he did while he was feeling trapped?

Take a large sheet of plain paper. In the middle of your paper, draw a picture of a lonely pit full of mud and mire.

You let me stand on a rock with my feet firm, and you gave me a new song, a song of praise to you. Many will see this, and they will honour and trust you, the Lord God. You bless all of those who trust you, Lord, and refuse to worship idols or follow false gods. You, Lord God, have done many wonderful things, and you have planned marvellous

things for us. No one is like you! I would never be able to tell all you have done.

- What do you think it feels like to stand on something good and solid in a storm or when it's icy or by the sea?

Draw the king when he's been pulled out of the pit, standing firm on the rock.

Sacrifices and offerings are not what please you; gifts and payments for sin are not what you demand. But you made me willing to listen and obey. And so, I said, 'I am here to do what is written about me in the book, where it says, "I enjoy pleasing you. Your Law is in my heart."'

- What can we give to God to please him?
- What could Jesus give to God?

Draw the expression on the king's face.

When your people worshipped, you know I told them, 'Our Lord always helps!' When all your people met, I did not keep silent. I said, 'Our Lord is kind. He is faithful and caring and he saves us.' You, Lord, never fail to have pity on me; your love and faithfulness always keep me secure.

- What sort of people help you?
- If you were speaking to friends at school, what would you choose to tell them about God?

Extra ideas

Bus stop

You'll need several dice, chairs, 'bus stop' signs (optional), hooter or whistle.

 Put the children in groups of four or five with a dice and stand each group in a queue at a chair which represents a bus stop. (You could put a 'bus stop' sign on it.) The aim of the game is to be at the front of the queue when the bus arrives. They take it in turns to throw the dice, and move up the queue one space if they throw a higher number than the person before, and down the queue one space if they throw a lower number. If they throw the same number as the person before, they stay where they are.

After a time limit decided by you, hoot the hooter or blow the whistle to show that the bus has arrived. The winner in each group is the one at the front.

Say that just as everyone was trying to get to the front of the queue, pushing other people out of the way to get there, so some people live their lives, always putting themselves first and shoving other people out of the way.

Parables

Read 'The two builders' (Matthew 7:24–27) and 'The two sons' (Matthew 21:28–32). These are both parables about doing what God wants.

Read out the parables while the children mime the actions. Give each group five minutes to think of a modern setting for the parable and to act it out to everyone else.

Daniel

Look at the story of the fiery furnace in Daniel 3. Shadrach, Meshach and Abednego choose to do what God wants even if it means being thrown in a fiery furnace. You could watch the *VeggieTales* video, 'Rack, Shack and Benny', which tells this story.

Paul

Read Acts 21:10–15. In this passage, Paul knows that it's the right thing to go to Jerusalem, even though it means he will be killed. You could act this out, with Agabus, Paul and some disciples playing the different parts.

Jonah

This drama, based on Jonah 1:1—3:3, is about Jonah, who really, really, really doesn't want to do what God wants. Jonah tries to go his own way, but God convinces him to do the right thing and save the people of Nineveh from punishment.

Characters: God, Jonah, Captain. (Other people can be sailors miming rowing, being tossed about in the storm, hauling on ropes and helping the captain to throw Jonah overboard.)

God stands in the centre. Jonah is to one side, playing with a Gameboy. The Captain is on the other side, behind a chair, which is the side of the boat. He is hauling in the anchor.

GOD: Jonah!

JONAH: Ummmm… Jonah who?

GOD: Jonah!

JONAH: Jonah Johnson, would that be? Or Jonah Jones? Very nice chap, Jonah Jones.

GOD: Jonah!!

JONAH: You mean, this Jonah? You mean me?

GOD: *(Pointing to Nineveh)* Yes! I want you to go to the city of Nineveh and tell the people there to stop doing wrong things and start doing right things. Then I won't have to punish them.

JONAH: *(Ticking them off on his fingers)* Go to Nineveh… tell them they're doing it wrong… I think you must have got the wrong Jonah, Lord. I think Jonah Jenkins would be much better at that than I would. I'll just go and fetch him, shall I…?

GOD: *(Pointing to Nineveh)* Jonah. Go to Nineveh.

JONAH: Me. To Nineveh. Fine! Great! Smashing! Nineveh it is! Nineveh, here I come! *(Points)* It's this way, isn't it? Well, I'll just be off then. To Nineveh.

Jonah starts walking very slowly towards Nineveh. He checks God isn't watching, then turns and heads in opposite direction at top speed—running on the spot.

JONAH: Catch me going to tell them off in Nineveh! Not on your life!

Nasty foreign place! They'd fry me in oil! They'd pickle my toenails in ketchup! They'd cut me in quarters and throw me in the crocodile pit! Nineveh? Not me! I'll get as far away from it as possible. Oy! Captain! Are you heading that way, towards Nineveh?

CAPTAIN: No, you landlubber, I'm heading that way. Away from Nineveh.

JONAH: This is the boat for me! *(Climbs over chair)*

GOD: I can see we're going to have to do this the hard way.

God blows. Captain and Jonah start being thrown about as if a great storm is rocking the boat.

CAPTAIN: I've never known a storm like this before!

JONAH: Rats! It's all my fault!

CAPTAIN: Why?

JONAH: I should be going to Nineveh, but instead I'm running away from God! Chuck me overboard and save yourselves!

CAPTAIN: Right you are. *(He pushes Jonah overboard)*

JONAH: *(As if swimming and struggling in the waves)* Here I go… Goodbye world! Argh! I'm drowning! There's seaweed round my head! I've swallowed a jellyfish! I'm in the middle of the Mediterranean Sea! I'm going to die! And now there's a hideous fishy monster coming towards me… It's got its mouth open… All those teeth… It's about to swallow me … I'm gonna die!

Jonah lies down with his eyes shut, then sits up and looks around him.

JONAH: Hmmm. I'm not dead! I can breathe. I can stand up! *(He does so)* I'm alive! It's a bit squishy in here… a bit fishy in here… But I'm alive! Praise God! It's a miracle! Thank you, God! Hooray for God! Three cheers for God!

GOD: He can stay there three days, just so he gets the message. And now…

JONAH: Whoa… here we go… u-u-u-u-up and away!

He mimes being thrown up by the fish and landing with a bump on the beach.

JONAH: Ouch! I smell of fish sick. Yuk!

GOD: Jonah…

JONAH: Oh, hello again, Lord.

GOD: *(Pointing to Nineveh)* Get up and go to Nineveh and tell the people to stop living bad lives and start living good lives.

JONAH: Nineveh? *(Points)* That's that way, isn't it, Lord?

GOD: It certainly is.

JONAH: OK, Lord. Whatever you want. Nineveh, here I come! *(Turns towards Nineveh and all freeze)*

You might like to ask the children some of these questions:

• Was Jonah being selfish by running away from Nineveh?

- Why did God give him a second chance?
- When was the last time you did something you knew was wrong?
- How does it feel to have a second chance, with God's forgiveness?
- How do we know when God wants us to tell somebody how much he loves them?

Prayer

Bible-based prayer for each other

 We always pray that God will show you everything he wants you to do and that you may have all the wisdom and understanding that his Spirit gives.

COLOSSIANS 1:9

Find a model of a house (for example, from Lego or Monopoly), something to represent school (like a book) and an empty circle (like a hoop or a ring). Place them in front of you and have everybody sit in a circle.

Explain that the house stands for our home and family. The book represents school and the ring is the world outside our own lives. Explain that you're going to pass round the three items and, as each person takes each item, they can ask God quietly, in their own mind, if there's some special thing he'd like them to do in that place. Explain that God sometimes speaks to us in an idea that comes into our minds, or a picture in our imagination that seems very real, or he might wait and speak to us later.

Before you pass round the objects, pray the prayer from Colossians: 'I pray that God will show you everything he wants you to do, and that his Spirit will help you understand how to do it.' (Older children could pray this prayer to each other as they pass the objects round.)

Response prayer

You could give out the leader's lines on cards so that different children can read them out.

LEADER: Even when I don't feel like it…
ALL: **Your will be done.**
LEADER: Even when it costs a lot…
ALL: **Your will be done.**
LEADER: Even when I think my ideas are better…
ALL: **Your will be done.**
LEADER: In our homes and families…
ALL: **Your will be done.**
LEADER: In our schools..
ALL: **Your will be done.**
LEADER: In our country…
ALL: **Your will be done.**
LEADER: All over the world…
ALL: **Your will be done.**

Imaginative prayer

Set the scene by saying that sometimes, for Christmas or birthdays, we might make a list of what we want—a wish list of presents.

If God were making a list of what he wants, what might be on it?

Either write his list or draw the things that he might want for the world, for the lives of the people you know, for you.

Talk about what's on the lists and draw them together with a simple prayer like 'Our Father, thank you that you want what's good for us all. Help us to understand what you want and to do it.'

Songs on the theme of God's will

 We've got the power (*Great Stories and Songs*, Unit 2, BRF)
May the mind of Christ my Saviour (MP 463)
Lord of all hopefulness (SHF 902)
For I'm building a people of power (MP 151)
Don't build your house on the sandy land (JP 39)

Graft and art

Opposites pictures

 Give each child a large piece of paper. Fold it in half, lengthways, widthways or diagonally. On one half write 'What God doesn't want' and on the other half write 'What God wants'.

The children can draw their ideas on each half. They might take just one idea (for example, God doesn't want war—he does want peace) and draw a large picture of just one scene on either side. Or they might design it like a match-'em-up puzzle with lots of little cameo pictures that are the opposite of the ones on the other side.

Working together jewellery/badges

When we pray 'Your will be done', we're not just sitting back and letting God get on with it. We're becoming part of the answer to our own prayer by cooperating with God.

As a sign that you want to work together with God, you could make a pendant or a badge out of ovenbake or airdrying clay.

Make your design and then carefully cut it in half so that you have two pieces that fit together. When they're baked and finished, you can wear one half and pin or glue the other half on to a bookmark for your Bible, to remind you that you are working in partnership with God.

Paper chain people

To show you're working with God and for other people, make a chain of people. Fold a piece of paper like a concertina and draw a person shape on the top, making sure the hands touch the edges. Cut out the person through the whole thickness of the folded paper, but don't cut through the hand joins. Open it out and decorate the different people.

Ongoing wall display

This session's picture is of Jesus praying in Gethsemane. You will find the template on page 124.

5

Give us today our daily bread

Get your bearings

I really like this bit. Jesus goes straight from the enormous sweep of God's kingdom and his divine will on to lunch. For him, there's no divide between religious stuff and day-to-day stuff. This is a good thing for us earthbound creatures.

This phrase of the Lord's Prayer is two things: a request that God will give us what we need to live, and a statement of faith that he does and has and will. When we pray this, we're saying that God gives us the food that we need to keep us alive: ultimately he, not the supermarket—or even the earth—supplies what we need. Jesus tells us to ask for our daily bread (not our daily chocolate eclair) —enough to satisfy us for the present.

Of course, our 'daily bread' is not just food to keep our bodies going, but food to keep our souls and spirits going too. Jesus asks us to realize and acknowledge that every good thing comes from God. God's kingdom is one of provision and plenty—of a healthy, balanced, nutritious diet, if you like.

In this session, we think about God giving the staple food of bread, and we try to understand more about the 'staple food' for our souls and spirits.

It's worth being forewarned that, in some churches, this session may throw up the question of children and communion. My group were straight in there: 'Why can't we have bread and wine at communion?'

Why not decorate your space... YELLOW?

Yellow is the colour of corn and ripeness and fruitiness. It's sunny and bright and has overtones of gold, so it feels rich too. You could include corn on the cob (tinned sweetcorn if the worst comes to the worst) and ears of wheat if it's the right time of year.

Quiet space

Possible objects and pictures for focus:

- Different sorts of staple food—bread, rice, pasta, potatoes
- Pictures of famine
- A Bible
- Pictures of people giving to others in different ways
- A church
- A calendar
- Squares of coloured felt
- A globe
- A heart
- A cross
- A light

Say, 'We've thought about "Our Father in heaven, hallowed be your name. Your kingdom come, your will be done on earth as in heaven". Today we're thinking about "Give us today our daily bread".'

> ✳ I wonder which colour felt you would choose for 'Give us today our daily bread'?
> ✳ I wonder which object or picture you would choose to go with 'Give us today our daily bread'?
> ✳ I wonder what picture is in your mind when you pray this part of the Lord's Prayer?
> ✳ I wonder why Jesus put this into the Lord's Prayer?
> ✳ I wonder if it reminds you of any stories?
> ✳ I wonder who 'us' is?
> ✳ I wonder why Jesus asks us to pray for something that God knows already that we need?
> ✳ I wonder why Jesus says we should pray for 'our daily bread' for 'today'?
> ✳ I wonder how God feels when we ask him to give us what we need?
> ✳ I wonder which object or picture he would choose to go with us?
> ✳ I wonder if we could leave out this part of the Lord's Prayer and still have all the prayer we need?
> ✳ I wonder what you like best about this part of the Lord's Prayer?

> ✳ I wonder how you would pray this part of the Lord's Prayer with just your hands?

Spend a moment asking God to give us our daily bread.

Take the square(s) of felt that the children have chosen and the pictures or objects they chose and place them on display for the rest of the session.

Either choose from the activities below or give the group the opportunity to do their own work to explore this part of the prayer, based on the wondering questions. Supply art and craft materials if you choose the second option.

Ice-breakers

Grab!

For this lively game you'll need about twenty small objects (beanbags or balls of rolled-up newspaper work well), four trays, and a whistle or hooter.

 Divide the group into four equal teams and give them a 'base' each in a corner of the room.

Give each team five balls. The team should put all its balls on to a tray in front of them.

The idea of the game is to get as many balls for your team as possible within one minute. One runner per team is chosen per round. At the whistle, the runner goes to the other teams' trays and steals one ball. S/he then takes it back to her/his own team's tray, then goes to grab another.

Meanwhile, of course, the other runners are stealing balls as well. Runners can only steal one ball at a time. Team members cannot do anything to stop their balls being stolen.

Count up the balls at the end of a minute. Keep scores if you want to.

Make sure each team starts off with five balls again. Swap runners from each team and play until everyone has had a go at running.

At the end, say that sometimes we behave in life like we did in the game—we try to grab more than we need and other people are left with nothing as a result. In today's part of the Lord's Prayer, Jesus teaches us to pray for our need, not for our greed.

What we want or need

Designate one end of the room WANT and the other end NEED. As you call out the following items, the group decide which end to run to, depending on whether they consider the object as something they just want or something they really need.

- Toffee fudge ice cream
- Vegetables
- Latest Disney DVD
- Chocolate
- Air
- Cola
- Bread
- Water

- Warmth
- Roller blades
- Clothes
- Latest fashion
- Holiday in the sun
- Bible
- X-Box
- TV

Talk about the difference between wanting something and needing it. When Jesus tells us to pray, 'Give us today our daily bread', is he telling us to pray for what we want or what we need every day? What other things beside bread do we rely on God to give us every day?

Puppets

You will need a glove puppet and some burger wrappers.

 Your puppet has turned into a zombie: he won't answer your questions or have any conversation. He's very robotic in all his movements. He just sits there watching his television, surrounded by burger wrappers. He's also very pale and unhealthy-looking. You discover that he's been doing nothing but watching junk television and eating junk food all week. You turn off the television and give him a good healthy apple to eat. You tell him he needs more than rubbish food and rubbish television to be a real person. Get the children to suggest what he needs to be healthy. The puppet realizes how silly he's been and resolves to be more sensible.

Bible exploring

Passages about
Give us today our daily bread

- Manna from heaven (Exodus 16:1–35)
- Feeding the five thousand (John 6:1–15)
- More than bread (Deuteronomy 8:3b)

Manna from heaven

This is a light-hearted retelling of the story of the manna from heaven, based on Exodus 16:1–21. (Manna actually means 'What is it?' in Hebrew!)

You could read the story or have some leaders perform it, reading in the different parts. Then let the children look at the original in Exodus 16:1–21, showing them the places on a map.

Have a quickfire quiz, with a scoreboard showing cut-outs of quails and loaves. Each correct answer scores a quail or a loaf for their team.

1. What country had the Israelites escaped from?
2. Who was the Israelites' (human) leader?
3. What did they start moaning about?
4. What did God send every evening?
5. What did God send every morning?
6. What happened if someone gathered too much and kept it overnight?
7. What was the manna like?
8. Did everybody gather the same amount?
9. Do we all need exactly the same things as everybody else today?
10. What does this story tell you about God?

Thingamajig from heaven

'We're hungry!' we wailed. 'Our bellies are empty!
Our tummies are hollow as drums!
Our stomachs are rumbling as loud as a lion's!
Oh give us some nosh for our tums!'

We all put the blame on old Moses, the boss,
And up went the grumbling cry:
'In Egypt we had all we wanted to eat
But out here we're all gonna die!'

The Lord God he whispered to Moses, the boss,
'They're not cross with you, but with me.
Relax—I'm in charge and I've got it in hand.
I'll provide lots of food, wait and see.

Just look in the evening and there on the ground
Will be oodles of meat for the pot.
And every morning you'll wake up to bread
Fresh for breakfast. You'll like it a lot.'

'We're out in the desert!' the people all sneered.
'You reckon this bread and this meat's a
Fast-food we order from over the phone?
Like ham, cheese and pineapple pizza?'

'Relax! God's in charge!' old Moses declared.
'You're gonna be fed—there's no question
Of starving out here. God knows what you need.
After all, who invented digestion?'

And lo and behold! We looked out of our tents
At sunset—what was that out there?
A whole flock of quail all flat on their backs
With their feet sticking up in the air!

Just like chicken nuggets but nicer by far.
We scoffed them for supper and tea,
And rose the next morning both fatter and glad
And, looking out, what did we see?

'What is it?' we yelled. 'It's not croissants or toast.
Not quite bun, not quite crumpet or cakes.
Not Shreddies. Rice Crispies? Or Frosties perhaps?
Or maybe it's holy cornflakes?

Oh what can we call it? How can we describe it?
Each flake is quite little, not big…'
'Let's call it just manna—that name will do fine.
It's Hebrew for thingamajig.'

The thingamajig looked like little white seeds
We thought we could try some and risk it.
And sure enough it was the yummiest stuff—
Tasting like honey-baked biscuit.

'Go get what you need!' called out Moses with glee.
'I said God would feed you—hooray!
Make sure you've enough, but don't stockpile the stuff.
Trust God to supply more each day.'

Well, some of us didn't do what we were told.
At the sight of the food we went barmy
And gathered enough for a week. And next day
It was maggoty, pongy and wormy.

But over the years we learned we could trust
That our needs would be met without fail.
As we walked with God we depended on him
For our thingamajig and our quail.

Our journey with God lasted forty long years.
Through the whole time he kept us all fed.
So we Israelites learned we could pray with true faith:
'Give us each day our daily bread.'

 Reproduced with permission from *The Lord's Prayer Unplugged* published by BRF 2004 (978 1 84101 262 9)

Feeding the five thousand

This is a retelling of the story from John 6:1–15, asking the children to play the parts of the people in it and to enter into it in their imaginations. You simply read the biblical account from John and pause at different points in the reading to ask the characters what they're thinking or seeing from their point of view. The questions given are simply suggestions—you'll certainly find other interesting questions to ask.

Ask everybody to imagine that they are people who lived when Jesus was about thirty, and that they all come from villages near Lake Galilee. Choose one person to be Jesus, some to be his disciples, including Philip and Andrew, and one to be a boy. The rest are people from round about who have heard about Jesus.

Ask several people, who should answer in character, 'What's your name? How old are you? What's your job? What do you know about Jesus?'

Read John 6:1–4. Ask Jesus and his disciples to sit together. Ask them, 'Have you been here before? Why have you come to this lonely place? Why do you like being with Jesus? What do you think your leader is planning to do out here?'

Read John 6:5–7. Ask the crowd to come and stand nearby. Ask Jesus and his disciples, 'How do you feel when you see all these crowds of people coming?' Ask Philip, 'How do you feel when Jesus asks you the question?'

Ask the crowd, 'Why have you come out here to this lonely place? How long has it taken you to get here? How long are you planning on staying?'

Read John 6:8–9. Get Andrew to bring out the boy with the picnic. Ask the boy, 'Why didn't you just eat your picnic yourself?' Ask Andrew, 'Why do you bother bringing this boy and his picnic to Jesus when it's so little?' Ask Jesus, 'How do you feel about this boy's generosity?'

Read John 6:10–11. Get everybody to act it out as it happened. Ask the crowd members, 'When did you last eat anything? Where do you think all this food has come from? What did you see Jesus doing from where you're sitting? How does it feel to be given all this free food?'

Read John 6:12–15. Get everybody to mime picking up the pieces and putting them in baskets. Ask Jesus' disciples, 'What are you going to do with

the leftovers now?' Ask the crowd, 'What do you think of Jesus after seeing this miracle?' Ask Jesus, 'Why are you running away to the hills on your own?'

Questions to follow.

Ask people to 'become themselves' again. Ask:

- Which moment in the story did you enjoy most?
- What did you find most surprising?
- Was there anything you found puzzling?
- What do you think this story has to do with 'Give us today our daily bread'?

More than bread

Ask the group if they remember what Jesus said to the devil when the devil tempted him to turn stones into bread.

Show them that this response was based on Deuteronomy 8:3b: 'People need more than food to live—they need every word that the Lord has spoken.'

This is a short sketch to illustrate the idea that human beings need more than food to live. After the group has had fun performing it, you could ask:

- Do you agree with Jarad?
- What sorts of things do we need to feed our souls and spirits?
- Where do we get them from?
- What did Jesus do to feed his spirit?
- What do you do to feed your spirit?

Characters: Burgle the alien, other aliens, Professor, Jarad

Burgle and the other aliens enter, pointing ray guns at the Professor and Jarad, who are backing away.

BURGLE: (To the Professor) Greetings, human being! We are aliens from Planet Qurgle. I am Burgle from Qurgle. We will not exterminate you if you tell us one thing for our research.

PROFESSOR: Certainly. Anything!
BURGLE: How do human beings work?
ALIENS: Yes! How do human beings work?
PROFESSOR: *(Whispering to Jarad)* Look, we'll keep this simple and perhaps they'll go away quickly and not kill us. Just keep quiet and do as I say. *(To aliens)* Welcome, alien friends from Planet Qurgle.
ALIENS: Greetings!
PROFESSOR: So you desire to learn how human beings work?

ALIENS: That is our desire.
PROFESSOR: A very good question. Here I have a specimen to show you.

Professor pulls Jarad into centre stage.

JARAD: Professor…!
ALIENS: Ah! It speaks!
PROFESSOR: Shut up, Jarad, you'll just confuse them. Remember— I'm trying to keep it simple! Now, my learned alien friends. The way a human being works is this. You open this hole… *(he opens*

Jarad's mouth)… and you insert fuel *(he puts in a burger in a bun)*.
ALIENS: Ah!
PROFESSOR: And the human being works. Simple as that.
BURGLE: This makes the human being work?
PROFESSOR: Absolutely. End of demonstration. Now off you go, and everybody stays alive and happy.
JARAD: *(Through the bun)* Oy!
ALIENS: Ah!
PROFESSOR: Shut up!
JARAD: But it's not as simple as that at all!
ALIENS: Ah!
BURGLE: You need different fuels?
JARAD: No! Yes! I mean…
PROFESSOR: A healthy balanced diet— carbohydrates, fibre, protein, vitamins…
JARAD: But not just that! Human beings need food to exist, but we need more than that to live!
ALIENS: Ah!
PROFESSOR: Shut up!
BURGLE: Tell us what you mean, human being.
JARAD: Well, human beings are more than just bodies that need food to keep us going. We need to feed our souls and our spirits as well, otherwise we'd be just like machines.
PROFESSOR: We'll be here all day explaining that!
ALIENS: What fuel do you need for your spirits and your souls?
JARAD: Different people need different things—beauty, ideas, truth, music, art, friends, family, science…
PROFESSOR: They'll never understand that!
JARAD: (Waves a Bible at them) But we all need the fuel of

 Reproduced with permission from *The Lord's Prayer Unplugged* published by BRF 2004 (978 1 84101 262 9)

	God's word to bring meaning into our lives.
ALIENS:	Ah!
JARAD:	And we need this sort of food (points to Bible) as much as we need this sort of food (points to burger).
ALIENS:	Ah!
BURGLE:	That is perfectly clear.
PROFESSOR:	What? You understand something so complicated?
BURGLE:	We understand that there is more to a human being than just a body.
PROFESSOR:	But…
BURGLE:	We will need to take some sample food from your planet. I will take this (picks up burger) and this (picks up Bible). We thank you.
PROFESSOR:	But…
ALIENS:	Farewell!
JARAD:	Simple really.

Extra ideas

The road to Emmaus

 Read the account in Luke 24:13–35 and draw a cartoon strip of what happens in it.

The parable of the friend needing bread at midnight

Read the parable in Luke 11:5–8. Modernize the story and act it out, with as much comedy as possible.

If your children ask for bread, would you give them a stone?

Read the story in Matthew 7:9. Improvise a conversation between a practical-joker parent who gives her or his children stupid things they don't want, and thinks it's really funny. Then improvise

another conversation showing how a good parent might react to being asked for things that her/his children need. Discuss which parent of the two is more like God.

Want and need

You'll need about twenty items as below.

Show the group about twenty items you might have on a journey, ranging from the essential (map, sleeping bag, food, water) to the frivolous (make-up, CDs, teddy bear, high-heeled shoes).

Ask the group to imagine they're about to set out across the desert on foot. They can only carry five things in their rucksack. What would they take and why?

When they have arrived at a consensus, point out that their choices were things they would need, not necessarily what they might want. Today we're looking at the part of the Lord's Prayer where Jesus tells us to ask God for what we need to live.

Ruth

The book of Ruth is a delightful picture of God's provision. Ruth is an outsider with nothing to call her own. She throws herself totally on the generosity of the rich and powerful Boaz. Boaz's eagerness to provide for her is a vivid reflection of God's generosity when we come to him with no resources of our own. As the story is set at harvest time, in the fields and on the threshing floor, it fits in beautifully with the theme of daily bread.

In the end, of course, God doesn't just provide Ruth with enough to eat. In the long run, she marries Boaz, has a son and starts off the family which eventually leads to David and to Jesus! So God provides for today and for eternity.

This is a simple script that tells part of the story. The group could read it or act it out.

Characters: Ruth, Naomi, Boaz, Nathan, workers in the cornfield

NAOMI:	Oh dear! Oh me! Oh my! *(Sobs)*
RUTH:	*(Putting her arm round her)* Naomi, what is the matter?
NAOMI:	I thought, when we got to Bethlehem, all our worries would be over. But now we're here, and we haven't even got a crust of bread to eat! *(Sobs)*
RUTH:	Don't cry! I'm sure God will look after us somehow. Tell you what, I'll go and pick up some leftover grain in one of the fields after they've harvested it.
NAOMI:	Praise God for his good laws that let poor people like us do such a thing! And praise God for such a good daughter-in-law as you, Ruth!
RUTH:	Right—I'll be off, then. *(Waves goodbye)*
NAOMI:	Look after yourself, dear! A young girl like you, all on your own…!
RUTH:	*(Looking around her)* Now, which field should I try first…? This one? Everyone looks very busy, hard at work.
WORKERS:	*(Swinging imaginary scythes and miming gathering up the grain)* Scythe, scythe, bundle, stack. Scythe, scythe, bundle, stack
RUTH:	Excuse me…

NATHAN:	*(Looking up from his work)* What?
RUTH:	I'm Naomi's daughter-in-law from Moab. My name's Ruth. We have no food. May I pick up some of your leftover grain?
NATHAN:	Not a problem, Ruth. Our boss, Boaz, he's very keen on making sure God's laws are kept, and as you can see, there's plenty of grain left for you to pick at. Go ahead. Follow the women.

Ruth follows the workers, miming picking up stalks of grain.

WORKERS:	Scythe, scythe, bundle, stack. Scythe, scythe, bundle, stack.

Enter Boaz.

NATHAN:	Here's Boaz now!
BOAZ:	The Lord bless you!
WORKERS:	*(Cheerily)* And may the Lord bless you!
BOAZ:	Good to see you all working so well. Don't forget to stop for a drink when you need one—it's very hot out here. *(The workers get back to work. Boaz turns to Nathan)* Nathan! The Lord bless you! You're doing a great job. Everything going all right?
NATHAN:	Oh yes, boss. Good harvest this year. God's been very generous.
BOAZ:	Plenty for us, plenty for the poor. Oh! I see we've got one already picking up her share. Who is she?
NATHAN:	Her name's Ruth, Naomi's daughter-in-law from Moab.
BOAZ:	Naomi—she was married to one of my distant relations. We'd better make sure Ruth is looked after well. Tell the men not to give her any hassle, Nathan. You know what some of them are like.
NATHAN:	Sir.
BOAZ:	*(Goes over to Ruth)* The Lord bless you, Ruth.

 Reproduced with permission from *The Lord's Prayer Unplugged* published by BRF 2004 (978 1 84101 262 9)

RUTH:	And may the Lord bless you, sir.
BOAZ:	I think it would be best for you not to pick up grain in anyone else's field. Stay here with the women and follow along behind them as they gather up what the men have cut. The men won't bother you. Whenever you're thirsty, you can drink from the water jars they've filled.
RUTH:	Why are you being so good to me, when I'm a foreigner?
BOAZ:	Aha! I've heard the gossip about you, Ruth. I heard how you left your own land to stay with Naomi. As you've thrown yourself on our God's protection, I pray he will reward you and bless you.
RUTH:	You're very kind…

BOAZ:	Look, it's lunch time—sit with us and share our bread. *(He mimes giving her a piece of bread, which she dips into a pot of sauce)* Take the leftovers back to Naomi. Nathan—let her take grain from wherever she wants. Leave plenty on the ground for her. And be nice to her!

WORKERS:	Scythe, scythe, bundle, stack. Scythe, scythe, bundle, stack.
NATHAN:	Right, everyone. Sunset! Time to go home!

Everyone waves goodbye and Ruth returns to Naomi.

RUTH:	Naomi! I'm back!
NAOMI:	How did you get on? *(Ruth opens up her sack)* Good heavens! I've never seen so much grain. You must have been to the field of someone generous. God bless the man who treated you so well! We've got more than enough to eat tonight. Praise God!

The last supper

Perform the account of the last supper in Matthew 26:17–30 as a dramatic reading. You'll need characters to read in the parts of narrator, disciples, Jesus, Judas. To avoid the dreariness and inadvertent comedy of chanted chorus lines, it's best to give the disciples' joint lines to one or two characters before you start. And because it's a solemn passage, it's worth practising before you go for the final version.

Afterwards, hot-seat any characters who are willing to be put in the hot seat.

Hot-seating is great fun and very easy. The actors remain in character and sit in the special chair you have designated as the hot seat. When one person is in it, the rest of the group has a time limit, set by you, in which to ask him questions to find out about what happened during the last supper. So they might ask Judas, 'What had you been plotting with the priests? How could you do that to your best friend? How did it feel when you realized Jesus knew what your plans were?' They might ask one of the disciples, 'What was it like eating the bread when Jesus had said it was his body?' And so on.

Make sure you praise each person for their efforts in the hot seat—it does require an act of imagination and there is an element of risk..

I am the vermicelli that gives life

Prepare some empty speech bubbles. Bring in books about food in different parts of the world. Say that, for us, bread is one of our 'staple' foods—it's something that most people in our country use as a basic food. But in other countries, there might be something different from bread that is the staple food.

Ask the group to use the books to find out what the staple foods of different countries are. Then draw pictures of children from those countries with speech bubbles that say, for example, 'Jesus is the spaghetti that gives life'; 'Jesus is the rice that gives life'; 'Jesus is the potato that gives life'. (I hope you won't end up with 'Jesus is the Big Mac that gives life' but who knows…)

Prayer

Prayer from Philippians

I know what it is to be poor or to have plenty, and I have lived under all kinds of conditions. I know what it means to be full or to be hungry, to have too much or too little. Christ gives me the strength to face anything.
PHILIPPIANS 4:12–13

Prepare the passage from Philippians 4:12–13 by writing it out, one phrase at a time, on smiley faces cut out of card or drawn on paper plates:

I know / what it is / to be full / or hungry, / to have too much / or too little. / Christ gives me / the strength / to face anything.

Ask everyone to think of a time when they've moaned about not having something they really want (but don't really need).

Read out the verses and say that Paul wrote them while he was in prison. Say that this is a great passage to help them out when times are tough, so you're all going to learn it!

Jumble up the smiley faces and get the group to put them in the right order.

Turn one of the faces over and get the group to

say the verse. Then gradually turn over more and more, repeating the verse each time until they can say it without any help from the smiley faces.

- Say sorry to God for being greedy.
- Thank him that he's given us the secret of being happy all the time.
- Say the verse together.

I am the bread that gives life

It would be a shame to do a session on bread without actually eating anything, but the obvious caveats about food allergies apply.

'I am the bread that gives life! No one who comes to me will ever be hungry.'
JOHN 6:35

Say that one of the things the first Christians did was to 'break bread together' (Acts 2:42). This showed that they enjoyed being together. It was an act of sharing and showing they cared about each other.

Find a really yummy fresh loaf of bread and invite the group (with clean hands) to feast their eyes on it, smell it, listen to the sound of it being cut or broken, touch the piece you give them and finally to taste it. Get them describing what they are seeing, hearing, smelling and so on. Encourage them to enjoy using all their senses to the full as they feast on the bread. Say that Jesus wants us to enjoy feasting on him just as much as we enjoy seeing/hearing/touching/smelling/tasting the bread.

Finally, pass round the bread, inviting each person to break off a piece for the person next to them. When everyone has a piece, ask them to hold it as prayers are said.

Invite the group to thank God for the good things that he gives us to eat, then eat the bread quietly together.

What about the starving?

You'll need newspapers and pound coins.

Collect newspaper cuttings about parts of the world where people are starving. Talk about the fact that God uses us to provide for people in need. Mention the proverb 'Throw your bread upon the waters and it will come back to you.' Say that you're going to 'throw some bread upon the waters' now, by trusting each of them with a pound.

Give each member of the group a pound and ask them to use it in some way that will increase it.

For example, they could buy some ingredients and bake something to sell (with a parent's help), or they could buy some seeds, let them grow and sell the seedlings for a profit, or they might buy a bottle of squash and sell drinks to the church family after a service. Spend some time discussing ideas and enthusing about it. Make it clear that you're taking part too.

It might be wise to send the pound home with a letter explaining the plan, so that parents can help!

Ask the children to bring back the pound and any extra by a given deadline and give it to a charity that helps people in need.

Songs about bread or God's provision

I am the bread of life (MP 261)
Jehovah Jireh, my provider (MP 354)
A boy gave to Jesus (JP 1)
Someone's brought a loaf of bread (JP 220)
Have you got an appetite? (SHF 746)
More than oxygen (SHF 927)

Craft and art

Making bread

If you have time, you could make normal bread with yeast. Remember to refer the group back to the kingdom parable of the yeast from 'Your kingdom come'!

If there isn't time, you could make unleavened bread, and tell them about the unleavened bread at the first Passover as you do so.

This recipe is from BRF's *Step into the Story* by Margaret Spivey and Anna Jean.

You'll need 225g plain flour (half white, half wholemeal), quarter tsp salt, 1 tbsp vegetable oil, water to make stiff dough.

Knead ingredients well together, roll into a thin rectangle, cut into squares, place on a greased baking tray and prick with a fork. Cook at 180°C/ 350°F/Gas Mark 5 for about 20 minutes until brown.

Or you could set a bread maker to have the bread baked at an appropriate time, and then have fun with different sandwich fillings. (Bread straight from an oven or breadmaker is tricky to cut into slices. Try to leave it to stand for at least half an hour, letting the smell waft tantalizingly round you all…) Who can make the most inventive sandwich —and eat it?

Suggestions for fillings: chocolate spread, jam, marmalade, yeast extract, ham, tuna, mustard, pickle, crisps, cheese, tomato, celery, lettuce, ketchup, HP sauce, butter…

Toast rack recipes

Make a cardboard toast rack for the display board and encourage the children to write 'recipes for life' on index cards to slot into it. For example:

Full life

Ingredients: God, love, a selection from the following—family, friends, music, stories, dreams.

Method: Put God in the centre of your life. Pour in generous helping of love from human beings. Add other ingredients and mix well. Allow space for questions. Watch life to grow and change. Enjoy!

God provides

Prepare plenty of pieces of paper cut into the shape of slices of bread. Children can either draw, write or cut out pictures from magazines and paste them on to the slices. Ask them to show on each slice of bread one good thing that God provides for us. You might want to limit it to types of food, or you might widen the theme to take in any good 'nutritious' things like the Bible, friends, sunshine, music and so on.

Ongoing wall display

Today's picture is of a loaf of bread.
You will find the template on page 125.

6

And forgive us our sins as we forgive those who sin against us

Get your bearings

How many times have you, like me, enjoyed a secret snigger as the traditional and modern versions of the prayer get mixed up between trespasses and sins and we ask God to 'forgive us our trins…'?

Forgiveness is right next to our food—it's as if Jesus knows that two-way forgiveness is as crucial to human beings as beans on toast. Perhaps it's his realistic acceptance that now we have put all our material problems into God's hands, we can turn our attention towards our spiritual needs.

Here Jesus asks us to pray for peace between God and us and between each other. We become aware of our own shortcomings and our need for forgiveness. But of course Jesus knows that the only way we can possibly understand God's forgiveness is by forgiving others with the same generous grace that we ask him for. This is another aspect of God's kingdom of peace, the never-ending forgiveness of real wrongs, which always involves sacrifice on the part of the one forgiving.

Children might misunderstand this line, and think that God only forgives us if we forgive other people. Of course, God's forgiveness is unconditional. Hooray! What we are saying in the prayer is that we believe in forgiveness so much that we are prepared to act it out in our lives as well as pray about it.

In this session, we have fun with Jesus' parable of the unforgiving servant, look at what the cross means, and the story of the paralysed man. And there are plenty of opportunities to pray for forgiveness and for help to forgive.

Purple is a 'sorry' colour—the colour for Lent and Advent, which are traditionally times when Christians take stock of life, concentrate on discipline and turn away from wrong things in their lives. Asking forgiveness is part of the process, as is a deliberate act of forgiving. Purple is also the colour of the robe that was put on Jesus to try to turn him into a mock emperor on Good Friday. You could use black grapes in your décor.

Quiet space

Possible objects and pictures for focus:

- Water
- Soap
- Something dirty and something clean
- People holding hands and hugging
- Squares of coloured felt
- A church
- A globe
- A heart
- A cross
- A light

Run through the prayer so far and remind the group that today you're looking at 'Forgive us our sins as we forgive those who sin against us'. Lay out the objects that you have chosen.

- I wonder which colour felt you would choose for 'Forgive us our sins as we forgive those who sin against us'?
- I wonder which object or picture you would choose to go with this part of the prayer?
- I wonder what picture is in your mind when you pray this part of the Lord's Prayer?
- I wonder why Jesus put this into the Lord's Prayer?
- I wonder if it reminds you of any stories?
- I wonder how God feels when we ask him to forgive us?

- I wonder which object or picture he would choose to go with us?
- I wonder which object or picture he would choose to go with the people we need to forgive?
- I wonder if we could leave out this part of the Lord's Prayer and still have all the prayer we need?
- I wonder what you like best about this part of the Lord's Prayer?
- I wonder how you would pray this part of the Lord's Prayer with just your hands?

Spend a moment asking God to forgive us our sins as we forgive those who sin against us.

Take the square(s) of felt that the children have chosen and the pictures or objects they chose and place them on display for the rest of the session.

Either choose from the activities below or give the group the opportunity to do their own work to explore this part of the prayer.

Ice-breakers

Scapetrolley

You'll need lots of balloons, and a pushchair, pram or trolley per team.

This game is to introduce the idea of removing sins, like the scapegoat.

Give each team the same amount of blown-up balloons, and stand them at one end of the room. One member from each team stands at the opposite end with a pin (or big boots). The team's aim is to get rid of all their balloons—but this can only be done by putting them in the trolley one at a time and taking it in turns to transport them to their team's popper, who can pop them however s/he wants to.

Only one balloon can be transported at a time, and players are not allowed to touch it as they travel. If the balloon falls out of the trolley on the way, the trolley journey has to start again from the team base.

You may want to ask if the children know what a scapegoat is. It's come to mean someone who is blamed when things go wrong. But originally it was a goat used on the Jewish Day of Atonement. The priest would put his hand on the goat's head and confess all the sins of the people, symbolically 'laying the sins' on the goat. Then the goat would be driven out into the desert and set free far from the camp so that it couldn't return. You can read about it in Leviticus 16.

Washing

You'll need some really dirty pieces of clothing—football shorts after a muddy match, a ketchupy T-shirt, stained socks and so on, and some handwashing powder, bowls or warm water. It might be an idea to have some stain remover as well.

Challenge the group to get the garments clean without using any water. Of course they won't be able to do it.

Then give them bowls of warm water and soap powder and teach them how to wash clothes by hand (a useful life skill anyway!).

Then talk about the way water can get rid of dirt and how, sometimes, our lives get in a mess and need cleaning up. The Bible sometimes uses the picture of dirt to describe bad things in our lives, and the Bible also describes how we can get clean again. This part of the Lord's Prayer helps us understand what it means to be forgiven and to forgive other people.

Puppets

You will need a glove puppet.

 Your puppet won't talk to you. When you eventually persuade him to tell you what the matter is, it turns out that you hurt his feelings by playing with someone else yesterday instead of him. You ask how it feels to be so grumpy and he tells you it feels horrible—like a big black cloud crushing him. Say that if he can forgive you, it'll feel a lot better. You say you're very sorry for hurting his feelings. He tries forgiving you and it does feel better! You have a big cuddle and you're friends again.

Bible exploring

Passages about *Forgive us our sins as we forgive those who sin against us*

* The cross (Luke 23:32–43), especially 'Father forgive them…'
* The man through the roof (Mark 2:1–12)
* The unforgiving servant (Matthew 18:21–35)

The cross

This story, based on Luke 23:32–43, was inspired by a story from Susan Lacy's *Stories to help you pray*, published by BRF.

Ask the children to sit or lie comfortably and to close their eyes so that they can picture the events of the story as you read it.

✳✳✳

 I'm Asiel. I'm eleven. Have you ever been mad and glad at the same time? I was! You see, our house had been burgled. And they'd taken away loads of my family's things. And my necklace! The one my grandfather left to me. That was what made me mad.

But the burglars had been caught. We didn't get any of our stuff back, but today I was going to watch them get what they deserved! And that was what made me glad.

So I ran into the city streets to watch. It was so busy in the city. Passover, you see—loads of Jews in Jerusalem from all over the world. It was so busy, no one noticed when I took a bunch of grapes from a market stall and ran off with it into the crowd.

We'd all come to watch the execution. Always a good laugh. My two thieves, and some other bloke, were going to get nailed up where they deserved. There were crowds lining the streets, watching the procession of soldiers and crooks going up the road to Skull Hill—shouting, throwing things at them, tripping them up as they stumbled past. It was good to see someone else so miserable.

I was so mad, thinking about what they'd nicked, I shouted the worst names I could think at them, and yelled all the chants with the crowd, and spat at them as they went past. I threw all that anger at losing my necklace on to the three crooks carrying their wooden posts up the hill. I even chucked some rotten grapes at them. It made me feel better, blaming them.

They got to the top of the hill. The Roman soldiers, of course, looked as if they'd seen it all before and just wanted to get it over with as quickly as possible. They flung the wooden posts down on the ground, where they bounced and rolled a bit. While I ate my grapes, they nailed signs on the posts which said what the three men were getting killed for. 'For nicking my necklace!' I thought bitterly. Then the soldiers tied a cross piece across one end of each post, with practised knots, and dragged the crooks over to them. They threw one man down on each and nailed them on. Then they hoisted the crosses upright and dropped them into a hole in the ground so they stood straight and we could see the three criminals die the slow deaths they deserved.

Two of the men—the two thieves who'd nicked my stuff—were on either side. They were howling and screaming, sweating and swearing. The one in the middle was quiet. Silent. I was still mad at what they'd done to me. I didn't see why he should be so quiet. So I made my way to the front of the crowd and I threw the rest of my squishy bunch of grapes at him, as hard as I could. It hit him all right. And it made him speak.

'Father,' he gasped, 'forgive them. They don't know what they're doing.'

The thief on one side lifted his head and shouted out, 'Oy! You! Jesus! Aren't you the Great Rescuer?' He laughed. 'So rescue yourself from this mess! And rescue us while you're at it!' The man in the middle said nothing. But the thief on the other side hollered back, 'Belt up! Show some respect! We belong here—we nicked the stuff—we're getting what we deserve.'

'Too right you are,' I thought. 'You nicked my necklace.' I watched Jesus' blood dripping down from the mess of spikes on his head on to my bunch of grapes at the foot of the cross.

The thief kept on speaking: 'But this bloke's done nothing wrong.' He tried to look at Jesus, though it hurt him to make any movement—the nails would see to that. 'Jesus,' he wheezed, 'remember me when you come into your kingdom.'

Kingdom? I squinted up at the sign on the middle man's cross. It said 'Jesus of Nazareth, King of the Jews'. Some king, I thought.

Jesus was turning, as far as he could, to the thief. 'Trust me,' he gasped, 'today you'll be with me in paradise.'

I shouted out, 'No he won't! He nicked my stuff! He's a crook! They won't let him anywhere near paradise! It's good people like me who get into paradise!' And Jesus' eyes turned from the thief to the bunch of grapes on the ground. He couldn't possibly know where they'd come from. But I suddenly thought, if I'd been caught stealing, maybe I'd have been nailed to a cross just like the other thieves. That's where I deserved to be. Then Jesus looked down at me.

And I didn't want to shout anything else. I didn't want to speak out loud. I just wanted to whisper one thing to that man on the cross.

***

After the story, ask the children to sit up when they're ready. You could ask some of the following questions:

- Who had hurt Asiel, the girl telling the story?
- What did they deserve?
- Whom did Asiel hurt in her turn?
- What did she deserve?
- Whom had Jesus hurt?
- What did he deserve?
- What did Jesus say to God when people hurt him so much on the cross?
- What does 'forgive' mean?
- What expression do you think Jesus had when he looked at the girl?
- What do you think might have been the one thing that Asiel wanted to whisper to Jesus?
- The thief had done terrible things, but Jesus still said that he would go to paradise. Is there anything that God can't forgive?
- Is there anything you can't forgive?

The man through the roof

There is a verse version of this story in *The Gospels unplugged* and another version in *Stories to help you pray*, both published by BRF.

You'll need an illustrated Bible or Bible story book, map of the Holy Land in New Testament times, a mat, a Bible, microphone (optional), and camera (optional).

Show the children pictures of New Testament scenes from an illustrated version of the Bible. Show them on a map where the village of Capernaum is and explain that if Jesus had called anywhere home, it would probably have been Capernaum.

Ask each child to imagine that they are a person living in Capernaum in the time of Jesus. You will need a few Pharisees, a paralysed man (give him the mat), his four friends and Jesus. Everyone else can be a villager.

Ask everyone to think what their name is, how old they are, and what they do most of the time. Are they at school, working from home, working as a carpenter, potter, ploughman…?

At this point, you can take round your real or imaginary microphone and ask several people what their name is or what they do for a living, until you feel that most people are happy with the game.

Say that you're going to read out a story from Mark's Gospel, and you're going to pause at various points. When you pause, could they please imagine where their character might be and what they might be doing at that moment and put themselves into that position, so that it looks like a photograph of that particular moment.

For example, if you said, 'It was early morning in Capernaum and everyone had gathered at the well to have a good gossip…' you might push a chair into place as the well, and all the characters would gather round and stand frozen in position as if they were chatting to each other.

You then take your microphone and ask a few characters what they're talking about, or what they're thinking about, or what they can see around them.

When everyone has got the idea, you can start reading the story from Mark 2:1–12.

You may like to pause after verses 2, 3, 4, 7, and 12. Each time you pause, and after the 'photograph' has been built up, go and ask questions like 'Why are you here? What do you think of Jesus? How do you know him? What do you think of what he's just said? How do his words make you feel? What can you see from where you're standing?'

If you have a camera, you could take an actual photo of each scene and turn the sequence into a 'photo-story', with thought and speech bubbles for the different characters.

After you have completed the story, ask:

• If disease can make our bodies paralysed, what can make our souls paralysed?
• How might we feel if our soul can't work properly?
• How can we 'get better' from this sort of 'illness'? (Look at verse 5.)

The unforgiving servant

For younger children, there is a version of this story in *Dragons and Monsters*, published by BRF.

The script below can be used to read out, act out and have fun with. It is based on Matthew 18:21–35.

*** * ***

Characters: Rosie, Sarah, Sam

Rosie is wearing a drab pinny, flicking a feather duster round the room.

SARAH:	Mu-um! Mu-um! Guess what Sam did! He took my *MegaHits* CD again!
ROSIE:	Give it back and say sorry, Sam.
SAM:	Here. Sorry.
SARAH:	That's not good enough! Every time he takes it he says sorry. And then he goes and takes it again! It's not fair! You should take his pocket money away for a week!
SAM:	Oh yeah? Well, what should Mum do as you've borrowed my CD player without asking *again*? I only borrowed one CD from you, but you took my whole CD player! Shouldn't Mum take away your pocket money for a year?
SARAH:	Well, how many times should I let you off?
SAM:	How many times should I let you off?
ROSIE:	Oooh! I think I feel a story coming on.

Rosie tears off apron and throws away feather duster to reveal ultra-cool clothes. She puts on wraparound shades and poses.

SARAH/ SAM:	Wow, Mum!
ROSIE:	Listen up, kids, this story's hot.
	Trust your mum, you'll like it a lot.
	It's a story from the master— the big JC.
	You want to join in? Rap with me!
SARAH:	There once was a king whose subjects owed
	Him loads and loads and loads and loads…
SAM:	And loads and loads…
SARAH:	…Of money! So
	He shouted, 'Come on! Pay me what you owe!'
ROSIE:	Sidney owed a massive amount,
	More piles of gold than you could count.
	He'd written so many IOUs
	They stretched from here to Timbuctoo.
SARAH:	Sid couldn't pay if he worked his whole life.
	The king said sadly, 'You'll have to sell your wife
	And your kids and your house and your cute little pet
	In order to repay this mega-debt.'
SAM:	Sid gave a howl and fell to his knees.
	'Oh mighty king, be patient, please!
	I'll pay you if you'll give me time Don't sell my gerbil!'
ROSIE:	That don't rhyme.
	But never mind! The king felt sorry.
	'I'll let you off your debts— they're cleared, no worry!
	I'll tear up every IOU letter.
	You can go free—no longer a debtor.'
SARAH:	Sid bowed low and dashed off grinning,
	Free from debts! A new beginning!
SAM:	But there stood Rodney, a bloke

	he'd bought
	Some chips last night. Sidney caught
	Him round the neck. 'Aha! Now Rod!
	Pay me back or go to quod!'
	Rod fell to his knees. 'Is it such a crime?
	I'll pay you back the money— just give me some time!'
ROSIE:	'Not likely!' said Sidney and dragged him off to clink.
	'When you can pay me what you owe, I'll set you free, I think.'
SARAH:	But other people saw the scene and very quickly set off
	To tell the king about it all. 'You know that man you let off
	His massive debt to you? Well, your majesty,
	He's thrown his friend in prison, for owing 50p!'
SAM:	The king went red with fury.
	'Bring Sidney here before me!
	You nasty little piece of work!
	You really do appal me!
	I let you off each penny of that massive debt you owed!
	But not a speck of mercy to poor Rodders here you showed!
	I reckon that it's safe to say, without a controversy,
	Since I'd been kind to you, you should have shown your friend some mercy!
	Call the jailer! Throw this man into the deepest cell
	Until his debt is paid. And throw his gerbil in as well.'
ROSIE:	The moral of the tale is clear: if Jesus forgives you
	The things you do that hurt him, can't you forgive others too?

***

- How is God like the king in the story?

Extra ideas

Debts!

*You'll need chocolate money (or toy/
Monopoly money if your budget's tight),
a pack of cards per group of four, pens
and paper.*

 This game is to introduce the idea of owing money and—perhaps—of what it feels like to be let off the debt.

Everyone has an equal amount of money. Each group shuffles and deals the cards.

Everyone turns up the top card of their pack. They then pay one coin to the player with the highest card (ace is low, king is high). The game continues. If they run out of money, they can write IOUs to carry on playing. When the last cards are turned up, the game is over and scores have to be reckoned.

Get the groups together and ask, 'Who owes money? Who is owed money? How does it feel?'

Perhaps one player would be able to pay her debt if she was paid what was owed her by another player. Perhaps everybody owes money to one player.

Ask what the player who is owed most could do if they wanted to—they could, of course, tear up the IOUs and write off the debt. Are any of them prepared to do that? How does it make the debtors feel?

But perhaps some aren't prepared to write off the debt. How does that make the debtors feel?

Explain that the debt has to be paid. You could invent some dreadful punishments that happen to debtors who default. But say in the end that, in this case, you're prepared to pay the debt from your own supplies to let the debtors off the hook. (Pay out the money owed.) How does that make them feel?

Say that the Hebrews had a great system: every seven years, they would have a 'year of Jubilee' when all debts would be written off and everyone could make a fresh start.

A conscience alley

Set up a conscience alley: ask the group to think of a situation where you find it hard to forgive somebody because they keep on doing the thing that hurts you.

Choose a good typical situation and ask one person to be the Decider. Half the group has to try to persuade the Decider to forgive that person. The other half tries to persuade the Decider not to forgive them.

Zacchaeus

Look at the story of Zacchaeus, who was forgiven by Jesus and it changed his life completely.

Esau

Look at the way Esau forgave his brother Jacob in Genesis 33.

Isaiah 53

Isaiah 53:4–6 has a powerful description of how much it hurts God when we do wrong things.

Did you know?

Jewish people still say 'Shalom' to each other as a greeting today. It means 'God's peace be with you'.

'Shalom' is a real wholeness of mind and body, and a real peace between you and other people and between you and God. Jesus died to give us 'shalom' in all those senses.

Prayer

The sponge cross

You'll need a plastic board (see 'Forgetto boards' in the Craft section), water-soluble marker pens, a sponge cut into the shape of a cross.

 Ask the children to write something they'd like to say sorry to God for on the plastic board—perhaps some way they've hurt someone in the last day or so.

Then say that when Jesus died on the cross, he wiped out all the wrong things we do, so that they simply aren't there any more. Use the sponge to wipe the board clean.

Psalm 51.1-12

You'll need one copy per person of the photocopiable sheet on page 116, highlighter pens, and felt-tips.

Say that King David knew what it felt like to do something that hurt other people and hurt God, and afterwards he wrote a song about it.

Read out the psalm once, then read it again very slowly, asking the children to doodle on their copies: they might like to highlight any words or phrases that they find interesting, puzzling or surprising. They might like to draw little pictures, patterns, or even simply colours of what the words suggest, around the song.

Give them some time at the end of your reading to think about it and draw some more.

Then it might be appropriate to ask them to talk about which parts of the song they find most interesting, or why they have drawn what they did.

Try to sum up what you've learnt about forgiveness from the song. Then read the psalm through all together.

Refuse collector

Imagine (or perhaps you don't need to imagine!) that your room is a complete mess. It's piled high with rubbish—broken toys, empty Coke cans, horrible screwed-up tissues, scraps of paper, mouldy apple cores and half-eaten toffees. You can hardly get to your bed at night. There's no room to play any games. It smells horrible.

You've had enough of it! So you get a big black bin bag and you pile in all the junk from your room that's cluttering it up. Picture yourself peeling those sticky toffees off the carpet, dumping armfuls of paper into the bag, dropping the tissues in one by one, clearing up that nasty broken toy that you always hated anyway. You push it all into the bin bag and tie up the top with the plastic tag. Then you carry it downstairs and put it out on the roadside. Just in time! Here comes the waste removal van. A man jumps out, smiles at you as you stand there, picks up your bag of rubbish, and throws it into the back of his van, then drives away, taking all your rubbish with him. You go up to your room. Wow! Doesn't it look fantastic?

Now imagine that all that rubbish is clogging up your life. Instead of sticky toffees, you can think of mean things you've said or done or thought, that have hurt other people. You feel bad about those things and you want to get rid of them. Picture yourself putting all those thoughts and words and actions into a big black bag and taking it down to the roadside. Picture Jesus driving up in a big van, smiling at you and saying, 'I've come to take away the sins of the world.' Picture him throwing all your rubbish into the back of the van, then driving away with it. All those horrible things have gone and you don't need to feel bad about them any more.

You might like to read what John the Baptist said when he saw Jesus coming up the road in John 1:29: 'Here is the Lamb of God who takes away the sin of the world!'

Songs to fit with the theme of forgiveness

 God forgave my sin in Jesus' name (MP 181)
Make me a channel of your peace (MP 456)
I'm accepted, I'm forgiven (MP 321)
Change my heart, oh God (MP 69)
O Lord, your tenderness (MP 511)
Create in me a clean heart (MP 108)
Bind us together, Lord (MP 54)
Shalom my friend (JP 217)
There is a redeemer (MP 673)

Craft and art

Forgetto board!

You'll need card, anything you like to decorate the cards, small sponges (you could cut up a big cheap one from a chemist's), a laminator or clear book-covering plastic.

 Say that you can get boards that you write on to help you remember things— we call them memo boards. But this board helps you forget things, so it's a forgetto board!

The idea is that you write on it something that you wish you hadn't said, done or thought and that you are sorry for; or something someone else has said or done that has hurt you. Then you ask Jesus

to forgive you and to help you to forgive the person who has hurt you, and you rub it off!

Decorate the edges of the boards, perhaps writing 'Forgetto' at the top, then laminate or cover with plastic so that they have a wipe-clean surface. Warn the children only to use washable pens to write on them.

Cross-stitch cross

You'll need something to stitch on (you can get sheets of plastic canvas from needlework shops, or wide-meshed canvas), wool in different colours, wide-eyed needles and scissors.

Cut out the plastic mesh in the shape of a cross, or, if using canvas, lightly pencil on the shape of a cross.

Remind the group that on the cross Jesus took away all the bad things we've done.

Give everyone a needle and ask them to make a cross stitch on the mesh cross to stand for each thing they are sorry for and would like Jesus to forgive them for. Then they can take another colour and make stitches for things someone else has done to them which they need to forgive.

You could either do this activity on one cross all together or give everybody their own cross to stitch.

Point out that the crosses you've sewn are also like kisses—Jesus loves you that much.

Cooking biscuits

Here's a simple biscuit recipe. This activity is just for fun. If you want to make a tenuous link with the theme, you could make a cross-shaped cutter from stiff card, or eat the biscuits ceremoniously at the end of the session and point out that just as the biscuits disappear without trace, so Jesus removes our sins without leaving a trace… hmmm.

Ingredients (for about 40 biscuits)

225g/8oz self-raising flour
100g/4oz castor sugar
100g/4 oz margarine/butter
1 egg, beaten
juice of half a lemon

1. Put flour and margarine in a bowl and rub in until mixture is like fine breadcrumbs.
2. Add sugar and mix thoroughly.
3. Mix in egg and enough lemon juice to make a stiff paste.
4. Roll out and cut into shapes.
5. Put on a greased baking tray and cook for 15 minutes at 180°C/350°F/Gas Mark 4.
6. Lift off and cool on wire rack.

Ongoing wall display

In this session there is the picture of the cross. You will find the template on page 125.

7

Lead us not into temptation

Get your bearings

While we're on the subject of forgiveness, Jesus reminds us to pray that we won't get ourselves into dodgy situations to begin with. He tells us to pray that we won't be tempted: it's a prayer that not only makes a request, but says, 'Oh dear, Lord, I know I'm a complete wimp when it comes to resisting temptation—I can't cope on my own. I know I need your help.'

I find it hard to get my head round the fact that Jesus was tempted just as we are. I have to remind myself that he didn't have it easy. He didn't hover about on a cloud, safely above the muck swilling round on earth. He knows what it's like to be tempted to take the easy way out, to wash his hands of the cynics, baddies and graspers around him, to put himself first, to give up when the going gets tough, to grab cheap pleasure. He knew that God his Father in heaven would guide him out of

danger and he wants us to have that confidence in God too. It's a theme that loops back into 'Your will be done'.

In this session we find out about Jesus' temptations in the desert and how he stood up to them. We also have a look at the way Joseph resisted temptation and think about how Jesus himself was tempted but never did anything wrong.

Why not decorate your space... GREY?

Grey reminds us of the stones Jesus saw when he was being tempted by the devil in the wilderness. We also talk about 'grey areas' in a question—the things that are neither completely right nor completely wrong. When we are faced with temptation, we need to make one decision or another, not stay in our grey indecision.

Also, grey is not a bright happy colour, but rather sombre and dull. It's a colour we might want to get away from quickly to something more positive.

Ideas to decorate your space might include stones, chunks of concrete, grey fabric and grey (silver) balloons.

Quiet space

Possible objects or pictures for focus:

- Stones
- Arrows pointing different ways
- Stone tablets of the Ten Commandments
- Pictures of different sorts of paths and roads
- Chocolate
- People holding hands
- Squares of coloured felt
- A cross
- A light
- A heart
- A globe

Run through the prayer so far and remind the group that today you're looking at 'Lead us not into temptation'. Lay out the objects you have selected.

---

* I wonder which colour felt you would choose for 'Lead us not into temptation'?
* I wonder which object or picture you would choose to go with this part of the prayer?
* I wonder what picture is in your mind when you pray this part of the Lord's Prayer?
* I wonder why Jesus put this into the Lord's Prayer?
* I wonder if it reminds you of any stories?

---

* I wonder if anyone has ever asked you to help them do the right thing?
* I wonder what difference it would make to the world if everyone tried to do the right thing?
* I wonder which object or picture he would choose to go with us?
* I wonder if we could leave out this part of the Lord's Prayer and still have all the prayer we need?
* I wonder what you like best about this part of the Lord's Prayer?
* I wonder how you would pray this part of the Lord's Prayer with just your hands?

Spend a moment asking God to help you do the right thing today.

Take the square(s) of felt that the children have chosen and the pictures or objects they chose and place them on display for the rest of the session.

Either choose from the activities below or give the group the opportunity to do their own work to explore this part of the prayer. Supply art and craft materials if you choose the second option.

Ice-breakers

What is temptation?

You'll need signs saying TRUE and FALSE, one at either end of the room, a chocolate bar, an advert for a car or similar.

 Say that 'temptation' is a funny word but it happens to us every day, so we're going to find out a bit more about it. As you read out the statement, the children decide whether it's true or false and run to the appropriate end of the room.

1. 'Tempt' means trying to make someone do something—usually something wrong. TRUE
2. Adverts on television tempt us to buy things. TRUE
3. I am tempted to eat this bar of chocolate. TRUE

4. So if I'm tempted to eat it, I have to eat it. FALSE
5. I am tempted to buy this car in the advert—it looks so beautiful. TRUE
6. So if I'm tempted to buy it, I have to buy it. FALSE
7. If we are tempted to do something wrong, we always have to choose to do it. FALSE
8. Jesus was never tempted to do anything wrong because he was so good. FALSE
9. Jesus knows what it's like to be tempted. TRUE
10. Everybody is tempted to do wrong things sometimes. TRUE
11. Saying 'No' to bad things we are tempted to do is always easy. FALSE
12. Jesus can help us choose the right thing to do, even if it's hard. TRUE

Sum up by running quickly through what you've learned in this game.

Pulled both ways

ROMANS 7:18–19, 24

I know that my selfish desires won't let me do anything that is good. Even when I want to do right, I cannot. Instead of doing what I know is right, I do wrong… What a miserable person I am.

This game introduces the idea of being pulled in two ways by our conscience and by temptation.

You'll need a sheet of newspaper, sweets, money or other bribes if using the non-violent version.

Ask for a volunteer—make sure it's someone robust, whichever version you use. Your volunteer's aim is to stay safe on the piece of newspaper—their island. He or she can choose a helper to be their anchor—someone who will help them stay on the island. The aim of the rest of the group is to try to get the volunteer off that safe island.

In the rough version of the game, the group can physically pull to try to get the volunteer off the island, while the anchor tries to hold them firm. Impose a time limit of 30 seconds. If the volunteer

stays on the island for that time, s/he has won!

In the less violent version, no physical contact is allowed, but the group can say anything they like—they can lie, they can offer bribes, they can make promises—anything to get the volunteer off the island. So someone might tempt the volunteer by saying, 'If you come off your island, I'll eat my socks.' In this version, the anchor uses persuasion to try to convince the volunteer to stay.

This may lead to an interesting discussion about how, sometimes, what we are tempted by turns out to be a lie or a cheat in some way. You may like to have some form of compensation for the disappointed volunteer, although consumption of footwear is not required by canon law, as far as I know.

Talk about how it feels to be pulled in two directions. Was the anchor any help? Read out Paul's experience, from Romans 7:18 above, of wanting to do right but actually doing wrong. Who was Paul's anchor? The next verse (25) says, 'Thank God! Jesus Christ will rescue me!'

Puppets

You will need a glove puppet.

 Your puppet is all on his own. Next to him on stage is a box of chocolates with your name on. He looks round carefully—no one can see him. He fights with his conscience for a moment, but it's too tempting. He secretly steals a chocolate and eats it. Then he steals another… and another… until he gets right inside the box and gets stuck. You arrive and have to pull him out. You might want to refer back to 'Forgive us our sins' as you forgive him for eating your chocolates. You ask him why he stole them—he tells you that they were just too tempting. You suggest that next time he might just turn his back so he can't see them any more, and walk away from them.

Bible exploring

Passages about *Lead us not into temptation*

- Jesus in the desert (Matthew 4:1–11)
- Joseph and Potiphar's wife (Genesis 39)
- He's been there! (Hebrews 4:15–16)

Jesus in the desert

Set the scene by showing the children pictures of the wilderness or desert where Jesus went for forty days, and read the account of it from Matthew 4:1–11. This may be very familiar to children who go to church regularly, so you could pause before key words or phrases as you read, and ask them to fill in what comes next.

Then read out this sketch between two of the desert pebbles. These could be manky grey sock puppets.

***

Characters: Sandy and Dusty (two pebbles)

SANDY: How long have we been lying out here in this desert, Dusty?

DUSTY: Ten thousand, three hundred and fifty-seven years, six months, three weeks, twenty-eight days, seven hours and four minutes.

SANDY: Five minutes now.

DUSTY: Ten thousand years of boredom! Out here in the heat and the dust! Never seeing any living thing!

SANDY: We saw a goat once, Dusty.

DUSTY: A dead goat, Sandy, a dead goat.

SANDY: Oh yes.

DUSTY: And as for people! Well! Who'd come out here?

SANDY: There was that bloke a while ago…

DUSTY: He was dead!

SANDY: No! Not him! You know… the one we recognized. Mind you, he wasn't far off dead. Looked as if he hadn't eaten for weeks.

DUSTY: Oh him! A good few centuries since we'd seen him at work! And there he was, just a stone's throw away! Yes, he was going through a bit of a rocky patch, in every sense of the word.

SANDY: And don't you remember, he picked you up…

DUSTY: His hands were filthy!

SANDY: Look who's talking. People who live in glass houses shouldn't throw stones, you know.

DUSTY: You what? Speak up, I'm stone deaf!

SANDY: Oh, never mind. And there was that horrible creepy voice, whispering to him.

DUSTY: Sent shivers down my strata, it did. The voice of someone with a stony heart. 'If you're really God's Son, turn these stones into bread.' I remember it clearly. Ugh.

SANDY: Mind you, you do look a bit like a bread roll.

DUSTY: Oh, thank you very much.

SANDY: And he really was hungry, wasn't he?

DUSTY: I thought I heard an earthquake. Turned out to be his tummy rumbling.

SANDY: But the thing is, knowing who he was…

DUSTY: What, him being the Great Maker, you mean? The Foundation Stone of the universe? From before the Stone Age?

SANDY: Yeah… he could have turned you into a bread roll, if he'd wanted to.

DUSTY: If you can make a world, I shouldn't think making a bread roll is very hard. Unless it's a stale one! Ha ha!

SANDY: That was terrible.

DUSTY: Rock bottom. Ha ha!

SANDY: So why didn't he turn you into a bread roll, if he was hungry? He just said, 'People don't live just on food but on every word that comes from God.' And he dropped you.

DUSTY: Ouch.

SANDY: He must have wanted to turn you into bread. And he could have turned you into bread. But he didn't turn you into bread. Wonder why.

DUSTY: Dunno. We'll have to puzzle it out. Leave no stone unturned. We've got plenty of time to work it out.

SANDY/
DUSTY: Ten thousand three hundred and fifty-seven years, six months, three weeks, twenty-eight days, seven hours and six minutes…

***

Ask what answer the stones might have come up with to the question: why didn't Jesus take the easy way out each time?

Joseph and Potiphar's wife

This is a dramatic version of Genesis 39:1–20.

***

Characters: Narrator, Potiphar, Joseph, Mrs Potiphar
Props: purse, hanky, cloak or coat for Joseph

NARRATOR: The story so far: Joseph has been sold by his brothers into slavery. He's been carried off on a camel to Egypt and sold to Potiphar, one of Pharaoh's officials. Potiphar soon learns that his new slave, Joseph, is a reliable, honest and hardworking chap, and he trusts him with more and more important jobs. Joseph begins to think life isn't so bad. But he hasn't reckoned on Mrs Potiphar getting a crush on him. Time after time she tries to tempt him to fancy her in return, but he always says no…

POTIPHAR: So Joseph, if you could take my gold down to the bank and choose a nice bunch of flowers for my wife…

JOSEPH: Of course, Master.

POTIPHAR: Excellent! I'll be in my study if you want to pop in for a quick drink before dinner.
(He goes off)

JOSEPH: Thank you, Master.

MRS P: Yoo hoo, Joseph!

JOSEPH: Yes, Madam. Can I help you?

 Reproduced with permission from *The Lord's Prayer Unplugged* published by BRF 2004 (978 1 84101 262 9)

MRS P:	Oh dear, Joseph. I seem to have dropped my hanky. Could you pick it up for me?
JOSEPH:	*(Picking up her hanky)* There you are, Madam.
MRS P:	Thank you. And Joseph…
JOSEPH:	Yes, Madam?

MRS P:	I seem to have something in my eye. Could you see what it is?
JOSEPH:	Let me see… No, Madam, can't see anything at all.
MRS P:	Don't you think my eyes are beautiful, Joseph?
JOSEPH:	Very beautiful, Madam. Now if you'll excuse me, I must go to the bank for your husband…
MRS P:	My husband who never does anything nice for me and who wouldn't notice if you were to just hold my hand… *(She grabs Joseph's hand)*
JOSEPH:	Madam! Really! I'm in a bit of a hurry! Please let me go!
MRS P:	Oooh, a good-looking man like you needs a beautiful woman like me to look after you.
JOSEPH:	But you're married to Mr Potiphar!

MRS P:	So what? Can't I tempt you to be a little more friendly? Aren't I the most beautiful woman you've ever seen, Joseph?
JOSEPH:	You are very beautiful, Madam, but my master, your husband, has trusted me with everything in the house except you, because you're his wife. How could I let him down? It would be a sin against God.
MRS P:	*(Catching hold of his cloak)* I won't take no for an answer. Kiss me, you hunk!
JOSEPH:	Aaaargh! Help!

Joseph runs away, but she holds on to the cloak.

MRS P:	I'll get even with you!
NARRATOR:	And she told lies about Joseph, so Potiphar had Joseph thrown in jail.
POTIPHAR:	You miserable slave! I trusted you with everything I had and you try to steal my wife!
MRS P:	That'll teach you to be so beastly to me, Joseph!

✳✳✳

Read the Bible version from Genesis 39:1–20.
  You could ask the group some of these questions:

- Do you think Joseph was tempted to say 'Yes' to Mrs Potiphar?
- How difficult was it to keep on saying 'No' to her?
- What stopped Joseph from doing the bad thing she wanted him to do?
- Do you think Joseph was cross with God when he was punished for doing the right thing?
- Who might try to tempt you to do something you knew was wrong?
- How hard would it be to say 'No' to them?
- Do you think anything bad would happen to you for doing the right thing?

He's been there!

Show the children the pictures of Jesus and ask them:

• What are the differences between the sort of life Jesus had as a child and the sort of life you lead as children in the 21st century?

• What sort of things would have been the same for Jesus while he was a child as they are for you?

It says in a letter in the Bible about Jesus: 'Jesus understands every weakness of ours, because he was tempted in every way that we are. But he did not sin!' (Hebrews 4:15).

• Do you agree that Jesus was tempted in every way that you are? Why? Why not?

• What difference might it make to know that Jesus had been in the same sort of situation as you, and he had chosen the good thing to do?

Some people wear bracelets or badges that have the letters 'WWJD?' on them. They stand for What Would Jesus Do?

Give out one of these 'tempting' situations per pair and ask the pairs to invent a believable conversation between the speaker and Jesus: What would Jesus do if he was still your age, living where you live, and someone said to him:

a) Here, why don't you have a cigarette? Everyone else smokes…

b) It won't hurt Kate if you join in a bit of gossip about her—she'll never know…

c) Go on, take these drugs. Only babies say no…

d) It doesn't matter if you cheat in the maths test…

e) Your sister won't notice if you take that Mars bar she's been saving…

f) Don't bother about being nice to that oddball in your class—he's someone else's problem…

g) Just copy your best mate's homework—the teacher won't notice.

h) Tell your mum you've done your piano practice already…

i) Don't tell anyone you go to church—they'll only laugh at you!

How easy would it be for Jesus to choose the right thing to say or do?

The letter goes on to say: 'So whenever we are in need, we should come bravely before the throne of our merciful God. There we will be treated with undeserved kindness, and we will find help' (Hebrews 4:16). How does that make you feel?

You might like to draw a picture of a thought you've had during this discussion.

Extra ideas

The worst place to be

This game introduces the idea of doing our bit to avoid falling into temptation.

 Put all the situation cards at one end of the room and all the place cards at the other end. The teams race up to get a card, one card at a time, then try to match the situation card with the most appropriate place card. The question to answer is: 'Where would  it be a bad idea to go?' A silly example: 'If you want to keep your clothes clean, it would be a bad idea to walk through a muddy swamp.'

After the game, talk about why it's a bad idea to go to those places, and what might tempt you to go there, even though you know it's a bad idea.

Think back to Genesis 3 and the story of disobedience. How did the snake tempt Eve?

Look at Hebrews 4:15–16. What do you like about these verses? Look at any of the following stories and decide who was tempted, how they were tempted, and what they chose to do.

- Abraham and Isaac in Genesis 22
- Ruth and Naomi in Ruth 1
- David and Bathsheba in 2 Samuel 11
- Jesus' would-be followers in Matthew 8:18–22.

Can you think of any others?

Prayer

God's promise

Learn 1 Corinthians 10:13:

God can be trusted not to let you be tempted too much, and he will show you how to escape from your temptations.

Incorporate this verse into a prayer. The children might read a line each and all join in on the verse repetition.

CHILD 1: Paul wrote to his friends:
ALL: God can be trusted not to let us be tempted too much, and he will show us how to escape from our temptations.
CHILD 2: When we are tempted to do something we know is wrong, help us say no. Help us to remember…
ALL: God can be trusted not to let us be tempted too much, and he will show us how to escape from our temptations.
CHILD 3: When someone tempts us to do something we know will hurt other people, help us say no. Help us to remember…
ALL: God can be trusted not to let us be tempted too much, and he will show us how to escape from our temptations.
CHILD 4: When we are tempted to do something just because everyone else is doing it, help us say no. Help us to remember…
ALL: God can be trusted not to let us be tempted too much,

and he will show us how to escape from our temptations.
CHILD 5: When we are tempted to be lazy, help us say no. Help us remember…
ALL: God can be trusted not to let us be tempted too much, and he will show us how to escape from our temptations.
CHILD 6: When someone tries to tempt us into danger, help us say no. Help us remember…
ALL: God can be trusted not to let us be tempted too much, and he will show us how to escape from our temptations.

Hand-round prayer

Pass a stone around the circle. As each child takes it, they can say a prayer, perhaps naming a particular thing they know they are tempted to do, and asking God to help them next time it happens. If they don't want to pray out loud, they can pray quietly and then pass the stone on.

Turning prayer

Read out this prayer with the group standing to face one direction—the 'wrong' direction. As you invite them each time to turn towards God, they jump round to face the opposite direction. Then, as the next temptation is named, they face towards the 'wrong' side again.

Dear Father God, when we are tempted to do something that hurts your feelings, help us to turn away from it.

When we are tempted to hurt other people to make ourselves look more popular, help us to turn away from it.

When we are tempted to take something that isn't ours, help us to turn away from it.

When we are tempted to be jealous of someone else, help us to turn away from it.

When we are tempted… (ask the children to suggest what they might be tempted to do).

Songs to fit the theme of resisting temptation

He who would valiant be (MP 224)
Thanks be to God (MP 637)
I want to walk with Jesus Christ (MP 302)
Stand up, stand up for Jesus (MP 617)
Will your anchor hold? (MP 770)

Craft and art

Stone painting

You'll need smooth stones for everyone, brushes, paints (acrylic paints look great, but poster paints will be fine).

Decorate the stones.

Shields

You'll need scissors, sticky tape, a variety of junk, card, plastic containers, missiles (scrunched-up paper balls), a prize.

Challenge the group to see who can make the shield that will withstand most missiles thrown at it and give its carrier most protection.

When they're all made, hold a contest and award a prize for size, lightness in weight, manoeuvrability, strength and general effectiveness.

Gates

You'll need paper and art materials.

Jesus talked about choosing the hard way, not the easy way, when he used the picture of gates in Matthew 7:13–14:

Go in through the narrow gate. The gate to destruction is wide, and the road that leads there is easy to follow. A lot of people go through that gate. But the gate to life is very narrow. The road that leads there is so hard to follow that only a few people find it.

Draw a picture of these two gates. How do you see them? Which looks more tempting?

Ongoing wall display

The picture for this session is a signpost pointing two ways. You will find the template on page 126.

8

Deliver us from evil

Get your bearings

Remember the haunting opening sequence of the film *Prince of Egypt*, where the Hebrew slaves, sweating over their bricks, sing the song 'Deliver us' with real guts? It's that passion to get as many miles as possible between us and evil that is squashed into this short phrase.

I wonder how Jesus felt when his disciples began praying the Lord's Prayer in his hearing. Perhaps he wanted to shake them and say 'Do you really want delivering from evil? Are you sure? Do you know how much it's going to hurt?' But by praying this phrase we're not only asking God to rescue us from all the bad stuff around us, but confessing that we know we need to be rescued: we can't go it alone.

It ties back to 'Your kingdom come'—a kingdom free of evil and with a king who protects his people against enemies from within or outside.

In this session, we look at the resurrection as the

ultimate in rescue plans, and see how much it costs to deliver us from evil. There's the amazing rescue across the Reed Sea—and I can't resist putting in Psalm 23, which has comforted so many people in situations when they've been in the valley of the shadow of death. Or you may want to look at the pattern of death and resurrection that recurs throughout the Old Testament.

Why not decorate your space... with STRIPES!

Stripes are a fabulous symbol for this session, reminding us of prison bars, of the coexistence of good and evil, of the rainbow of colours that God sent Noah as a promise that he would never again destroy the earth by a flood, and of the price Jesus paid to deliver us from evil—the cruel stripes of the whip across his innocent back.

Think along the lines of stripey wallpaper, rugs, blankets and fake fur (not many mentions of tigers and zebras in the Bible, but who are we to quibble?).

Quiet space

Possible objects and pictures for focus:

- A rainbow
- A lifeboat
- An ambulance
- A police car
- A fire engine
- A tunnel
- A letter
- Key and padlock
- Pictures of dangerous situations: war/hazards/disasters and so on
- Someone keeping another person safe
- Squares of coloured felt
- A cross
- A globe
- A light
- A heart

Run through the prayer up to this point and ask the children who knows what comes next. Lay out the objects you have selected.

> * I wonder what 'deliver' means in the Lord's Prayer?
> * I wonder which colour felt you would choose for 'Deliver us from evil'?
> * I wonder which object or picture you would choose to go with 'Deliver us from evil'?
> * I wonder what picture is in your mind when you pray this part of the Lord's Prayer?
> * I wonder what sort of evil we are asking to be rescued from?
> * I wonder why Jesus put this into the Lord's Prayer?
> * I wonder if it reminds you of any stories?
> * I wonder how God delivers us from evil?
> * I wonder what God has already done to deliver us from evil?
> * I wonder how it feels when God rescues us?
> * I wonder if he wants us to rescue other people from evil?

> * I wonder which object or picture he would choose to go with us?
> * I wonder if we could leave out this part of the Lord's Prayer and still have all the prayer we need?
> * I wonder what you like best about this part of the Lord's Prayer?
> * I wonder how you would pray this part of the Lord's Prayer with just your hands?

Spend a moment asking God to rescue us, deliver us from evil in our lives, and to rescue his people round the world from the evil they are suffering under at the moment.

Take the square(s) of felt that the children have chosen and the pictures or objects they chose and place them on display for the rest of the session.

Either choose from the activities below or give the group the opportunity to do their own work to explore this part of the prayer. Supply art and craft materials if you choose the second option.

Ice-breakers

Escapology

 If you don't have a friendly escapologist you can rope in to demonstrate, try a home-grown version.

You'll need toilet rolls.

A volunteer is wrapped up like a mummy in the toilet roll. The end is left hanging free, not tucked in. The mummy's challenge is to escape from the wrappings without breaking the toilet roll within two minutes.

As a variation, you could make it a race between several mummies.

Hand tangle

Stand in a tight circle, facing inwards. Close your eyes and put your right hand in the middle, groping about until you touch another hand, which you then hold on to.

Don't let go! Repeat with the left hand.

Then open eyes. The group's challenge is to untangle themselves without letting go of each other's hands. You could follow this with a game of 'Stuck in the Mud' or 'Chain Tig'.

Puppets

You will need a glove puppet.

 This time your puppet is in bed and is scared. He keeps peeping out and ducking under the sheets again. You find him under the sheets, trembling. He's scared of monsters. He hates being on his own because there might be monsters. You say that God hates his people to be scared of anything. You ask the children how big God is—he's bigger than anything that might hurt us. You ask the children where God is—he's always with us. You say that the puppet might want to listen carefully to today's session as it might help him a lot.

Bible exploring

Passages about *Deliver us from evil*

- Resurrection (Matthew 28:1–10)
- Rescue from Egypt (Exodus 14)
- Psalm 23

Resurrection

You will need Bibles, a large sheet of paper per group, pens, and everyday objects that could be used as percussion instruments.

Read through the account of the resurrection in Matthew 28:1–10.

Make a copy of the graph on page 119 for each group. Ask them to 'compose' a 15-second piece of 'music' that tells the story they have just read, using only sounds.

So if they imagine that there was a bird singing in the first three seconds before the two Marys

arrived in the garden, they should write 'birdsong' in the vertical axis and put three 'x's by seconds 1, 2 and 3 from the time axis to show at what point this sound should be made.

They then continue filling in other sounds on the vertical axis (footsteps? weeping? earthquake? angel's wings? screams?), marking on the time axis when the sound comes in the piece.

To perform the finished piece, you quietly but clearly count out the seconds while they make the sounds at the appropriate moment. They may want to revise it after a first try.

Discuss what they see in their mind's eye as the different sound pieces are performed.

Ask what the resurrection has got to do with 'Deliver us from evil'. What has Jesus proved that he can rescue us from?

Rescue from Egypt

This response story tells of a time when God rescued his people from evil in a very dramatic way. Each time you say the words in bold, the children respond with the response you have taught them. It's great fun.

Teach the children the responses:

Egyptians: Yikes! *(bite knuckles in fear)*
Chariots: Neeeeow! *(watch chariot zoom past)*
Moses: Yo! *(punch air)*
Reed Sea: So deep! So wide! *(point down, then out to the sides)*
Israelites: Cluck cluck *(chicken wings)*
The Lord: Hooray! *(both hands up like Mexican Wave)*
Desert: Phew! *(wipe brow)*

✳✳✳

 We couldn't believe it! The **Egyptians** had kept us slaves all these years. And now, here we were, just walking away from them, rescued by **the Lord** and by his right hand man, **Moses**. Oh, we were still scared of those **Egyptians**—yes, we **Israelites** were chicken. We wanted to get as far away from Egypt as possible.

The Lord led **Moses**, and **Moses** led us

Israelites, and we **Israelites** followed **Moses** away from the **Egyptians**, round the **desert** towards the **Reed Sea**. And there we set up camp.

But oh horrors! Oh terror! The **Egyptians** changed their mind about letting us go. And they decided to capture us again. And they set out across the **desert** in their speedy **chariots**. We saw them coming towards us in their **chariots** in great clouds of sand, those **Egyptians**. Were we scared? No! After all, we were the **Israelites**. We weren't scared—we were TERRIFIED!

We groaned to the Lord and we moaned at Moses. 'Why did you drag us out here? We'd rather be slaves in Egypt than die in this desert!'

But **Moses** answered, 'Don't be afraid! Be brave and you will see **the Lord** save you today. These **Egyptians** will never bother you again. **The Lord** will fight for you and you won't have to do a thing.'

And **the Lord** told **Moses** to stretch out his stick across the **Reed Sea**. And that's what he did. And in front of our eyes, **the Lord** sent a great wind to blow back the **Reed Sea**. The **Reed Sea** opened up and we **Israelites** tremblingly walked through on dry land with a wall of water on either side.

And when the **Egyptians** saw what had happened, they jumped in their **chariots** and charged after us. But **the Lord** made their **chariots** stick in the mud. And while they were still stuck, **Moses** stretched out his arm again and the **Reed Sea** crashed down on top of the **Egyptians** and swept them all away.

And that is the story of how **Moses** rescued us **Israelites** from the **Egyptians** with their **chariots** and led us through the **Reed Sea** and out into the **desert** to safety in the power of **the Lord**.

***

Ask:

• What do you think it felt like to be a slave to the Egyptians?
• What do you think it felt like to walk out of Egypt safely?
• What do you think it felt like to see the Egyptians coming after you again?
• What do you think it felt like to see the soldiers who were about to kill you getting washed away?
• What sort of things might we be slaves to today?
• How does God rescue us from them?
• How does that feel?

Psalm 23

You'll need the cartoon strip outline on page 120, photocopied on to A4 paper, one copy per child.

Say that King David (the one who nobbled Goliath) used to be a shepherd and knew all about rescuing his sheep from danger. He noticed lots of things about God that reminded him of a shepherd. So he wrote a song about God which has been a firm favourite with Christians for centuries.

Read the psalm through and ask the children which part most reminds them of 'Deliver us from evil'.

Ask the children to design an illustration for each frame of the cartoon strip.

Challenge them to learn the psalm by heart—it's only six verses long.

The opening sequence of the film *Prince of Egypt* shows the slaves labouring and plays the song 'Deliver us!' This would be a good introduction to this session's theme, 'Deliver us from evil'.

The big rescue picture!

Give a brief account of the story involving each of the Bible characters in the list below. As soon as the children have guessed which character you are talking about, write the name of that character on a piece of paper and put it where everyone can see it, but finish telling the story.

If there are some you're not sure of, use the references to look up the stories—it might help to have a children's Bible to hand, where the stories are in easily-recounted chunks.

Ask what all these stories have in common— they're all stories about being rescued from danger.

Ask the children in groups to choose one of the stories and practise acting it out. Watch the finished performances and talk about who was rescued, what they were rescued from, who did the rescuing and how they were rescued.

The stories are:

- Noah: Genesis 6—9
- Joseph and brothers: Genesis 37—45
- Moses in his basket: Exodus 2
- Reed Sea: Exodus 14
- Gideon: Judges 6—8
- Samson: Judges 16
- David and Goliath: 1 Samuel 17
- Esther: Esther 1—8
- Jeremiah in the dry well: Jeremiah 38
- Daniel in the lions' den: Daniel 6
- Jonah in the fish: Jonah 1—4
- Jesus' flight to Egypt: Matthew 2:13–15

- The woman caught in adultery: John 8
- Lazarus: John 11
- Resurrection: Matthew 28
- Peter in prison: Acts 12

Prayer

St Patrick's breastplate

This is a great prayer for children to learn and this version gives an action with each phrase, so it ends up almost like a dance. It's a 'deliver us from evil' prayer, asking Jesus to keep us safe and affirming our trust that he does.

Christ be with me
(hold your own wrists by almost folding your arms)
Christ within me
(both hands flat on chest)
Christ behind me
(both hands behind you)
Christ before me
(both hands in front of you)
Christ beside me
(one hand to each side)
Christ to win me
(hands clasped above head like Grand Prix winner)
Christ to comfort and restore me
(hands imitate rocking a baby, or hugging yourself)
Christ beneath me
(both hands point towards floor)
Christ above me
(both hands point upwards)
Christ in quiet
(hands together in praying position)
Christ in danger
(hands held up as if warding off danger)
Christ in hearts of all that love me
(with palms up, move arms outwards to either side to 'show' those around you)
Christ in mouth of friend and stranger
(bring hands back to centre)

Paper chains

You'll need newspapers, scissors, sticky tape.

Ask the children to find pictures or stories from the newspapers about the terrible things evil does in our world—war, famine, violence and so on. Older children could summarize the story briefly and say what sort of evil has brought about this bad situation. Greed? Selfishness? Laziness?

Cut up the newspaper pages into strips and tape the ends of the first one together to make a loop of chain. Make a long chain by linking the strips together.

Make it long enough for the children to hold the chain around them as they stand in a circle.

Say 'Our Father in heaven, thank you that you are a God who wants to rescue us from evil. We pray for the people who are caught up in evil and ask that you will deliver them too. Especially we pray for... (current example that the children might choose). As we break this chain now, let it be a symbol for us of your power to break the chains of evil in our world. And show us how we can play a part in freeing your people from their chains.'

Then everyone rips the chain and stamps on it as they shout 'Amen!'

Up, up and away!

You'll need scissors, and a helium balloon tied to a weight by as many pieces of string as you have children.

Say that Jesus tells us to pray 'Deliver us from evil' because he knows how much evil can tie us down and stop us doing what we were made to do—just as this balloon would really like to be soaring through the air, but it can't because it's tied down to this horrible weight by all these bits of string.

What might be tying you down and stopping you being the person God wants you to be? It might be something that scares you, or a bad habit, or something you've done that hurts God or someone else.

You're going to cut one piece of string to set the balloon free, and as you do, ask God to set you free from the thing that's tying you down. You can pray it quietly in your own head. One by one the children can cut a string and say their prayer silently until the balloon flies free.

If you don't have qualms about environmental issues arising from one balloon being released, you could do this prayer outside and cheer the balloon on its way. If you have tolerant bellringers and a nice, high church tower, you could let it go up the tower. But even going to the ceiling of the hall will be good fun.

Songs to fit the theme of rescue

The Lord's my shepherd (MP 660)
You are my hiding place (MP 793)
God's not dead (JP 60)
God is raising up an army (SHF 731)
Thank you for saving me (SHF 1015)
My God is so big (JP 169)

Craft and art

Jelly baby bondage

You'll need jelly babies, liquorice, strawberry laces or writing icing, plain biscuits such as digestives or rich teas, plain icing.

Imprison your jelly baby behind strawberry lace bars, then eat it to freedom!

Use the biscuit as a base and glue your jelly baby on with icing. Over the top of it, stick bars made from lengths of laces glued on with icing, or writing icing.

NB: The symbolism of this activity won't stretch too far!

Raft craft

A mini raft is a great image of safety in the midst of danger.

> *You'll need plastic straws, sticky tape, string, a large bowl of water (a baby bath paddling pool or large washing-up bowl would be ideal), assorted plastic dolls (for example, Barbies, Action Men, Kens).*

Ask the children to design and make rafts from the materials provided, that will float and bear the weight of as many plastic dolls as possible.

Make and test!

Flickbook

Make a flickbook of a lifeboat rescue by cutting and stapling the pages in order from page 121. You need to line up the left-hand edge and staple the pages at this edge with page 1 on top and page 9 at the bottom of the flickbook.

The children could then design their own flickbook, choosing a different person or animal to be rescued, to pick up on the theme of deliverance from evil. The simpler the picture, the more effective it will be.

Ongoing wall display

The picture for this session is
a key and padlock. You will find the template
on page 126.

⑨

For the kingdom, the power and the glory are yours, now and for ever

Get your bearings

I don't blame the early Christians for wanting to finish Jesus' prayer by focusing on God's glory rather than on evil. Although his prayer stops at 'Deliver us from evil', Jewish custom was to finish with a phrase of praise, and perhaps his disciples would have added one on without even thinking. It's a good uplifting way to finish, tying up lots of themes very exuberantly.

Again we have the mention of God's kingdom: we're asking God to bring this kingdom about in our own lives. We declare that God is powerful and can do all the things we have asked him for in our

prayer. And we acknowledge that he is glorious—a word that takes us out of our earthbound drudgery and into a realization of the beauty, might, and fizzingly ecstatic wonderfulness that make up God's glory, not just in the past but now and on into the future. It's an affirmation of faith that whatever happens on this earth, God will never change. It's like admitting how small and temporary we are in relation to his marvellous eternity.

In this session we catch a vision of heaven's glory through the passages in Revelation—sometimes these passages are the light at the end of the tunnel from our earthly perspective. We can also look further into God's glory through the dreams and visions given elsewhere in the Bible.

Why not decorate your space... BLUE?

In medieval pictures, angels and Mary are often dressed in blue, as it's a colour that represents heaven.

Postcards and travel agents' posters of blue sky and sea all raise the spirits and set the scene for the 'ideal kingdoms' we think about in this session.

Quiet space

Possible objects and pictures for focus:

- Objects from 'Hallowed be your name'
- Objects from 'Your kingdom come'
- Battery
- Pictures of powerful natural things like waterfalls, lightning, elephants, tornadoes, volcanoes
- Glitter
- Foil
- Sequins
- Squares of coloured felt
- A cross
- A globe
- A world
- A light

Say, 'We've nearly come to the end of the prayer. Today we're thinking about the ending that Christians added to Jesus' prayer a long time ago.' Lay out the objects you have chosen.

* I wonder which colour felt you would choose for this part of the Lord's Prayer?
* I wonder which object or picture you would choose to go with this part of the prayer?
* I wonder what picture is in your mind when you pray this part of the Lord's Prayer?
* I wonder why this ending was added on to Jesus' prayer?
* I wonder how you like to end your prayers?
* I wonder if it reminds you of any stories?

* I wonder why we pray this, when God already knows about his kingdom, his power and his glory?
* I wonder how God feels when we praise him?
* I wonder which object or picture he would choose to go with us?
* I wonder what you like best about this part of the Lord's Prayer?
* I wonder how you would pray this part of the Lord's Prayer with just your hands?

Spend a moment telling God what we think of him.

Take the square(s) of felt that the children have chosen and the pictures or objects they chose and place them on display for the rest of the session.

Either choose from the activities below or give the group the opportunity to do their own work to explore this part of the prayer, based on the wondering questions. Supply art and craft materials if you choose the second option.

Ice-breakers

Wonderful world

This is a quiet activity to inspire awe and wonder.

On the table, set out a number of natural objects that are marvellous in some way, like a fossil, a leaf, an apple cut in two, a pine cone, a precious stone, a twisted stick. Also have one object that has been made by someone.

Show the group the object that someone has made and ask them what they can tell about the person who made it, just by looking at it.

Ask the group to have a look and pass the natural objects round carefully, then to choose which one they think is the most marvellous. Take it in turns to say what it is about the object they have chosen that is so special. Ask if they can tell anything about the person who made these things.

Say that all these things are only tiny, tiny things that God has made for us to enjoy—they are only a fraction of the beautiful and wonderful world he has created. We are thinking in this session about how we praise God, and one way is through the wonder we feel about what he's made.

Wow!

Get hold of a few copies of the *Guinness Book of Records*, even if they're a few years out of date. Lots of families will have one, and charity shops may well stock a few if the worst comes to the worst.

Ask the group to find the most wonderful fact they can from the books. As they read out what they've chosen (it will probably be the most pierced body or the longest intestinal worm discovered, but never mind) take note of any expressions of awe (discarding the yuks and urghs).

Say that it's that sort of feeling that ends the Lord's Prayer—a wow!—as we think back over what God has done, will do and does every day for us.

Puppets

You will need a glove puppet.

 Your puppet is upset because of all the good things round him that only last for a little while. His dandelion clock is all puffed away, he's finished a delicious slice of cake, the flowers in the vase have died, his ice cube has melted in his drink. Isn't there anything that doesn't stop? You reassure him that the best things in life go on and on and never stop. Love goes on

for ever: even when people die or go away, you know you'll meet them again one day, and most of all, God's fantastic love for you started before you knew it did and will go on for ever and ever. You could show him your wedding ring if you have one: a circle goes on and on with no end or beginning, just like God and his love.

Bible exploring

Passages about *For the kingdom, the power and the glory are yours, now and for ever*

- Alpha and omega (Revelation 21:6)
- Praise him!
- Pentecost (Acts 2)

Alpha and omega

This activity highlights how Jesus is at both the beginning and the end (for ever and ever). Put a label up to show that one end of the room is the BEGINNING and the other end is the END.

The children are in pairs, A and B. A stands at one end of the room and B stands at the other.

You call the following and the pairs put their hands up to answer. If they are at the BEGINNING end, they give the start part of the answer, and similarly the END end gives the end of the answer.

a) **What is the beginning and end of the alphabet?**
(A and Z)

b) What is the beginning and end of the word CAT?

(C and T)

c) What is the beginning and end of the sentence 'I love my teddy'?

(I and teddy)

d) BEGINNING people only: What might the judge say at the beginning of a race?

('Ready, steady, go' or similar)

e) END people only: What does this sign mean?

(Show an 'End of motorway' sign)

f) BEGINNING people only: What does a green traffic light mean?

(Go)

g) END people only: What does a red traffic light mean?

(Stop)

h) BEGINNING people only: Here are two letters from the Greek alphabet: alpha and omega. Which is the beginning of the alphabet?

(Alpha)

i) END people only: Which is the end of the Greek alphabet?/Can you remember what the name of this letter is?

(Omega)

j) Everyone: Who said 'I am the Alpha and the Omega'?

(Jesus)

Praise everyone for joining in so well, and discuss:

• What do you think Jesus meant when he said, 'I am the alpha and the omega'?
• What do you think this has to do with why we say 'for ever and ever'?
• What else can you think of that lasts for ever?

You might find the alpha and omega carved on your font if you have an old one—take the children to see it, if you do. Alternatively, many churches have alpha and omega symbols on altar cloths or stained-glass windows. See what you can find!

Praise him!

This part of the Lord's Prayer is a shout of praise to God. How do some Bible characters praise God?

Photocopy either the reference or the whole verse of the passages below on to slips of paper (depending on how good your group is at reading).

Give the slips to half the group and make sure they can read what's on them or have found the verse in their Bibles.

Give the other half of the group slips of card with actions written on them.

The 'action' group children take it in turn to act out their action, and the 'verses' group try to decide who has the verse that is being acted.

Verses

When they heard that Jesus was coming for the festival, they took palm branches and went out to greet him. They shouted 'Hooray!'
JOHN 12:12–13

The angels who stood around the throne knelt in front of it with their faces to the ground.
REVELATION 7:11

David was dancing for the Lord with all his might...
2 SAMUEL 6:14

Moses and the Israelites sang this song in praise of the Lord...

EXODUS 15:1

Miriam, the sister of Aaron, was a prophet. So she took her tambourine and led the other women out to play their tambourines and to dance.

EXODUS 15:20

Shout praises to the Lord!

PSALM 150:1

Praise God with cymbals, with clashing cymbals.

PSALM 150:5

Actions

Waving
Kneeling with your face to the ground
Dancing
Singing
Playing a tambourine and dancing
Shouting
Banging cymbals together

Discuss whether the children like praising God themselves and how they like to do it. Would they enjoy using instruments? Ribbons? Dance? Is there anything you can do about taking their ideas on, like asking someone in to lead a workshop on dance?

Pentecost

There is a great link to Pentecost here, to show that the story of Jesus doesn't finish at Easter or Ascension Day, but that it goes on and on. The passage is also bubbling full of people praising God, just like this line of the Lord's Prayer.

Read the account of Pentecost below and ask the children to act it out as you read it—there are lots of actions in it for them to do. There's lots about people speaking in the passage, but they will need to act their speaking silently (or it gets a bit silly).

After they have acted it out, ask what this passage has to do with God's kingdom, God's power and God's glory and the way these go on 'for ever and ever'. Help the children to

understand that this was the moment when the Church was born and Christians realized they had Jesus' Spirit living in them for ever and ever.

✳ ✳ ✳

 It was the Day of Pentecost, the Harvest Festival for the Jews. All Jesus' followers were together in a room. There weren't very many of them. They were praying to Jesus. Some were kneeling, some were standing, some were sitting.

Then suddenly they heard a noise! It was coming from above them. It sounded like a strong wind blowing. They looked up in surprise. They looked round as the sound of the wind filled the whole house. They looked at each other—what was going on?

As they looked at each other, they all started to point at spots just above each other's heads. They could see what looked like flames settling on every person there!

Then whoosh! Like a shower of warm water, the Holy Spirit came into everyone and they began speaking in lots of different languages, all talking about the marvellous things God had done.

They were speaking so loudly and laughing

so loudly with the excitement of it all that the people outside heard them through the windows and the open door, and they started gathering round to listen. There were people there from all over the world. But all of them heard somebody speaking their own language! They could hear what wonderful things God had done!

The people outside scratched their heads and shrugged their shoulders. They asked each other, 'What does it all mean?' But some people pointed their fingers and shouted, 'They're drunk!'

So Peter stood up, and the other disciples stood with him, and Peter spoke to the crowd.

He told them about Jesus and they listened, and when they heard about Jesus dying on a cross, they began to cry. They asked Peter, 'What can we do?'

He told them to turn back to God and go and be baptized, then they would have the Holy Spirit too.

And do you know, about three thousand people believed Peter and were baptized that day! They were all really good friends, like a big family! All Jesus' followers sat and listened to Peter tell them even more about Jesus, and they ate lots of meals together.

But they didn't fit into one room now!

***

Prayer

Feather prayers

You'll need a bag of feathers (from craft or toy shops)—ideally red, orange and yellow ones so that they remind everyone of the flames at Pentecost—and a candle.

 Sit everyone in a circle. Have fun holding a feather on your hand, then blowing it towards a child, one at a time, until everyone is holding a feather.

Light a candle in the middle of the circle. Explain that you're going to read a bit about the Holy Spirit and then there'll be a short time of

quiet, when they can all listen in case God wants to say anything to them. Read Acts 2:1–4. After the silence, ask if anyone wants to say anything, then blow out the candle.

Crown praise

You'll need, for each child, a piece of gold card cut into points along one side to look like a crown, sticky tape, glittery stickers.

Remind the children of today's line of the Lord's Prayer. It talks about God's kingdom and power and glory—and we're all part of that kingdom! We're all princes and princesses in the kingdom, so let's make a crown to remind ourselves.

Place the stickers in the centre of the circle.

Ask the children to think of something powerful that Jesus or God did in the Bible or does today. For every idea the group comes up with, everyone can stick a sticker on their crowns.

Then ask if they can think of something glorious about Jesus or God. Again, for every idea, everyone gets a sticker.

Then remind everyone that the Lord's Prayer says God's kingdom lasts 'for ever and ever', so bend the crowns round into a circle, and show the children how the circle goes on and on without ending.

Stick the crowns into the right shape and size.

Stand in the circle, wearing the crowns, and say a short prayer: 'Thank you, God, that you are king and you are powerful and you are glorious and you go on for ever and ever. And thank you that we are princes and princesses in your kingdom. Amen.' (You may wish to bow and curtsey to each other.)

Dance it

You'll need ribbons (see 'Craft and art' below) and music.

Do the craft first and make ribbons to use in a simple dance. Put on a praise song from a CD or play it live, and ask the children to use their ribbons to worship God.

Choose a song that is uplifting and rhythmic— for example, 'He is exalted' or 'Teach me to dance to the beat of your heart'.

Craft and art

Ribbons

 These simple ribbons are great to use in worship songs. You may find the adults wanting to have a go too!

It may be appropriate to warn the children not to poke each other's eyes out, *before* you make them.

You'll need lengths of ribbon about 2m long, dowelling rod in lengths of about 15cm (from DIY wood department), swivels (from angling shops), needles and thread, sticky tape (ideally coloured), sandpaper.

Depending on the age of your group, you may like to do some preparation for this.

1. Sand the ends of the dowel rods so that they're smooth.
2. Trim the ribbon to stop it fraying.
3. Sew the ribbon on to one loop of the swivel.
4. Tape the other loop of the swivel on to one end of the dowel rod.

5. Decorate the dowel rod if you want to, with coloured tape.
6. The ribbon should now move gracefully and freely when you hold the handle and wave it.

Song writers

Ask the children to write their own song based on this line of the Lord's Prayer. Here's one way of approaching it:

Write 'For the kingdom, the power and the glory are yours, now and for ever' in the middle of a large sheet of paper.

Tell the children to forget, for the moment, about rhymes and rhythms, as you're going to scribble down lots of ideas for the song. What other words would they like to praise God with? Write down all the ideas.

Looking at all the ideas, are there any that suggest a rhythm on which you could base your song? For example, 'For the KING-dom, the POW'R and the GLOR-y are YOURS (rest). NOW and for-EV-er, a-MEN (rest rest).'

Practise clapping or tapping the rhythm you choose. Then see if it needs an answering rhythm and clap that one too. Do any of your ideas fit into the answering rhythm and make sense?

Build up your song, and start to experiment with possible tunes that fit your rhythm.

Rhyme can be fun, but it is a bit restricting, and you may find the meaning distorted ('Oh God you are so great / Even when to church I'm late...' yerg), so you may want to ditch the idea and concentrate on the meaning, rhythm and notes.

You may want to send the children off into small groups to practise their final versions.

Peephole theatres

This slightly more complicated craft activity picks up on the idea that this line of the Lord's Prayer gives us a peep into the praise of heaven, giving us a tiny glimpse of a greater glory. It takes a while to make the theatres.

You'll need shoeboxes, scissors, card, sticky tape, tissue paper.

Ask the children to choose one scene from the Bible that shows God's power or glory (for example, creation, calming the storm, Pentecost—there are so many to choose from!).

Cut a square from one end of the shoebox to look through, and cut out a hole in the top and on each side to light the scene. You may want to cover these holes with coloured tissue paper for added atmosphere.

Inside the shoebox, the children are going to make a silhouette scene of their chosen event, so they can use the card to make backdrops/flats and little stand-up figures which they stick into place, facing the opposite end of the box to the cut-out end.

Put the lid on and view the scene inside.

Make any additions or alterations and tape down the lid.

Songs of praise

 Come on and celebrate (MP 99)
Father, we adore you (MP 140)
I will raise my hands in praise and adoration (JP2 376)
We really want to thank you, Lord (JP 268)
Yesterday, today, forever (MP 787)

Ongoing wall display

Today's picture is the fire of Pentecost, a symbol of God's glory. You will find the template on page 127.

98

10

Amen and the whole Lord's Prayer

It's the Big Picture time! This session has lots of ideas for bringing together what we've learned about the Lord's Prayer. The idea is that our understanding and appreciation of Jesus' prayer will have been deepened over the time we've spent on it and now we can enjoy praying it more than ever.

The ice-breakers deal with what 'Amen' means and the rest of the session can be spent praying the whole prayer in whatever way you like.

Amen is a real 'Yo!' of a word. It's Hebrew, of course, and means 'surely' or 'truly'. It's the way a Hebrew would say 'I trust you for that' or 'I'll sign my name to that' or 'That's what I say too'. A short

way for children to remember the meaning might be 'I agree!'

I remember kneeling meekly at the altar rail for communion and receiving the bread with a discreet and Anglican 'Amen'. Then the student next to me answered the whispered prayer 'The body of Christ, broken for you' with a loud and confident 'Oh yes!'

That's what Amen is—a joyful affirmation of faith that God has heard our prayer and will answer it. There's a great bit in 2 Corinthians (1:20) that goes, 'Christ says "Yes" to all of God's promises. That's why we have Christ to say "Amen" for us to the glory of God.' It's good to think of Jesus sitting next to God the Father, listening to our prayers, nodding at God and saying, 'I'll second that, Dad.'

Why not decorate your space... MULTI-COLOURED!

Well, after all, it's party time—a good argument for making your space as bright and cheery as you can. The different sessions have been in different colours, so, as you bring them all together, make sure you have all the colours you included over the sessions. Add some white if you plan to use the 'Make space for the Lord's Prayer' activity on page 106.

Just to remind you—we've suggested green, black, orange, red, yellow, purple, grey, stripes and blue.

Ice-breakers

Trust games

 Amen is a way of saying 'I trust you to answer this.' Trust games introduce the idea of trusting someone else.

There are lots of variations of these games in drama books but simple ones include the following.

Stand behind your partner with your hands very near her shoulder blades. Your partner leans back slightly and you catch her and push her gently upright again. Next time, hold your hands up a little further away (only a few centimetres more each time), bracing yourself with one foot in front of the other, ready to take the weight. Keep going for as long as both partners feel confident to relax backwards or to catch safely.

One player stands in the middle of a group of four or five others, gathered in a small circle. The centre player closes his eyes and relaxes, while the other players gently push him from one to another. The centre player keeps his feet in one place and simply sways as he is pushed. It's very soothing!

Point out that you had to trust each other for these exercises to work—and we can show that we trust God by saying 'Amen' at the end of a prayer.

I agree!

Get groups to improvise or act out this scene. It's school and your class wants something from the Head. You, the leader, can be the Head. The group should decide what they might ask for. Then they should act out the scene when they go to his/her office. One of them needs to do the talking, but the others need to show that they all agree with the request.

Act it out and, at the end, ask what ways everyone used to show that they agreed with the spokesperson.

Say that when we say 'Amen' at the end of a prayer, it's a bit like that—we're saying that we all agree with the prayer and trust that God will answer it.

Puppets

You will need a glove puppet.

 Your puppet has the Lord's Prayer on bits of card and is trying to put them into the right order. You might talk with him about each phrase as you pick it up and remind him what situation he was in when he needed that phrase. You can admire together how Jesus puts them in a really good order. Then suggest that you pray the whole prayer all together with the group in one of the following ways.

Extra ideas

Walk the Lord's Prayer

 This takes a bit of setting up, but is great fun to do. It's taken from the idea of prayer labyrinths, as in Sue Wallace's book, *Multi-Sensory Prayer* (Scripture Union).

This is more of a prayer journey or prayer obstacle course, however, with the activities set up around the room. As a group, you walk together from one activity to another.

After you have done it together, the children

may want to do it on their own or lead their parents round.

The activities at the different points are mostly ones included in the individual sessions in this book: this is a way of bringing them all together, reminding the children what they have learned, and enjoying the prayer.

At each point, have the appropriate phrase of the Lord's Prayer written out clearly on a poster, and have the equipment ready set up. It would be good, but not crucial, to have a rug to sit on at each point, not only for comfort but also to define the area. (Not many households can rake up nine rugs, however—unless you're manic picnickers.)

As you finish each activity, make it part of the activity to leave the equipment as you found it, ready for the next group to use.

You may want to stick gaffer tape to the floor to lead from one activity to the next so that children can follow it if they're going to do it on their own later.

Explain at the start, 'We're now going to walk the Lord's Prayer together. At each point in the room, we're going to pray one part of the prayer. Please will you follow me to each point and, when we get there, sit down quietly, ready for what we'll do there. When we've prayed that part of the prayer, please follow me to the next part. We don't need to run, even if we're excited, because we're showing

God that we think he's worth taking time over.'

Pause for a moment and open a Bible and read from Luke 11:1–2, where it says, 'When Jesus had finished praying, one of his disciples said to him, "Lord, teach us to pray, just as John taught his followers to pray." So Jesus told them, "Pray in this way…"'

Now lead the children quietly to the first point and wait until they're all sitting down. Point to the poster and pray out loud together the words on it. Then do the activity for that point, tidy up, and move on to the next point.

Our Father in heaven

You'll need a large picture of a tree with GOD OUR FATHER written on the trunk, and pens.

'Let's write our names in God's family tree to show that we are all his children… And as we walk to the next point, let's hold hands* to show that we all belong to each other in God's family.'

(*Put hands on someone else's shoulder or omit completely if you have older children to whom holding hands is really naff.)

Hallowed be your name

You'll need a cross, and flame-shaped pieces of red and orange tissue paper in a basket or box.

'Let's take off our shoes and stand up to remind ourselves how holy God is. Now let's each put a flame in front of the cross to remind ourselves of the time God told Moses his name in the burning bush…

'Now let's put our shoes on again, ready for the next part of our prayer journey.'

Your kingdom come

You'll need a map of the world, and red hearts (foil from craft shops, or paper).

'Let's put a heart on the countries in the world that need God's justice and love and kindness to their people, especially their poor people and their children.'

Your will be done on earth as in heaven

You'll need a small cross and two nails.

'Let's pass round the cross and the nails to remind ourselves what it cost Jesus to do what God wanted instead of what he wanted.'

Give us today our daily bread

You'll need a selection of supermarket tins and packets as a display, and small bread rolls on a plate (use an alternative if you have wheat allergies in the group).

'Let's eat a piece of bread to remind us of all the food God gives us every day.'

Forgive us our sins as we forgive those who sin against us

You'll need a cross, a bowl of water, some squirty soap, a towel or paper towels.

NB: It's worth putting this station near a water source to make it quick to sluice away the dirty water and replace it with clean water.

'Let's take it in turns to wash our hands in the water to remember how Jesus forgives us and washes away the bad things we do or say or think. When we've washed our hands, we can look at the cross and think how Jesus died on a cross to take our sins away... Now I'm going to empty the dirty water away so that all that dirt is gone for ever.'

And lead us not into temptation

You'll need something to make a narrow opening, like a play tunnel or clothes horse with a rug over it, and something to make a wide opening, like two chairs or screens.

'Sometimes we have a choice between taking the easy, tempting way out, and taking the hard, right way out. Let's squeeze through the narrow opening to show we want to take the right way, even when it's harder.'

But deliver us from evil

You'll need a dark blanket, bowl of grapes, sweets or some other treat.

'I'm going to cover you with this blanket now—it sometimes feels like this when we're scared or in danger. But now I'm going to pull you out into the light again, just as God rescues us from bad times. Come and eat a sweet when you come out, just as God holds a feast for us in his kingdom... And to show how happy we are when God rescues us and treats us to a feast, we're not going to walk to the last point, we're going to conga.'

For the kingdom, the power and the glory are yours, now and for ever. Amen.

You'll need bubble mixture.

'Would you like to lie down here as we reach the end of our prayer journey? It's time to relax in God's love as we trust him to answer our prayer. Let's watch these lovely bubbles shine in the light as I blow them. Each time you pop one, you can say AMEN! as our beautiful prayer comes to an end.'

Move the Lord's Prayer

Ask the group to devise and learn their own movements for each phrase of the Lord's Prayer. They might be hand movements or whole body movements. Is this something they could teach the whole congregation in the next church service?

For a more adventurous group, they might like to dance it, using a musical setting like Cliff Richard's version (*The Millennium Prayer*).

Draw the Lord's Prayer

Cartoon

Photocopy the cartoon grid on page 122 for each member of your group. Ask the children to fill it with a cartoon of someone praying the Lord's Prayer, showing what they're thinking about each line of the prayer as they pray. You could also think about what God might be saying back.

Our Father in heaven

A variation on this is to use the grid to make a cartoon of the idea that someone is praying the Lord's Prayer without really thinking, showing what they are thinking instead. Talk about what might happen if God interrupted them and asked after each phrase what they really meant by that, or if they really wanted him to answer that prayer. Talk about how we might pray the prayer more carefully. (See 'Make space for the Lord's Prayer' on page 106.)

Doodle

Give everyone paper and pens/crayons. Say that you're going to read the Lord's Prayer through ten times, and while you're reading it, they can doodle whatever pictures come into their minds. Perhaps they'll remember some of the stories you've heard during the weeks and draw those. Perhaps they'll want to draw what we're asking God to do for us. Remind them that they need to listen to the words,

and try to see what pictures they suggest, not just scribble down what they feel like without listening. Give them time to finish, and listen to what they have to tell you about what they've drawn.

Book cover

You'll need this book, medieval Books of Hours, any prayer books.

Show the group the different book covers and illustrations for the prayer books. They may not know that Books of Hours were medieval books that rich people had made especially for them by artists, containing prayers and the words of the services.

They may like to look at the different ways the books of prayers are illustrated. What is the cover trying to say about the contents? Using them as inspiration, they could design their own cover for a book on the Lord's Prayer, *or* design a page with the Lord's Prayer on it, decorated in their own way.

The big picture

You'll need a very large piece of paper, felt tips or other coloured crayons.

Thanks to Peter Privett's for the basis of this idea. It's great because there's no wrong way of drawing, because it's a real act of togetherness, it makes you take time out to think slowly about the prayer, and it's fun.

Take a really large sheet of paper—as big as you can find. Sit the children round it on the floor. Have a supply of felt-tips to use.

a) Everyone draws a line on the paper in their favourite colour—just 'taking a line for a walk' from one side of the paper to another, as long or as short as you like, so that all the lines cross, twist round and make a network of shapes across the paper.

b) Then each person fills in a space near them with the instruction below. When they have all filled in their shape, everyone moves round the paper one place to the left and fills in another space there, and so on, moving round each time. You should end up with the whole paper filled up with a patchwork of different colours, shapes, symbols, pictures, doodles, letters, words…

Here are suggestions for what to draw.

- Some warm-ups: dots/stripes/spirals/zigzags
- Then some focusing ideas: something to do with you/something to do with someone who's on your mind at the moment/something to do with a situation that's on your mind at the moment
- Then each phrase of the Lord's Prayer in turn, finishing with 'Amen.'

If there are still spaces, ask the children to fill them in with anything they want to add to their prayer—people, places, requests, thanks, or perhaps just patterns and pictures they would like to include.

Admire the finished result. Ask if anyone wants to talk about the things they drew or the way the picture turned out.

Then pray the Lord's Prayer slowly, looking at the big picture as you pray.

(You could draw a circle in the centre to start with, leaving the circle empty until the end. Then ask, 'I wonder what should go in the centre of our prayer picture?' and draw in what the children suggest.)

Write the Lord's Prayer

Have a look at these versions of the Lord's Prayer. Ask the group if they could write their own version, with the same meaning but completely in their own words, like these people have done. They might like to write a version that would be special to a refugee, a prisoner, or some other particular person.

If you have children who are interested in different languages in your group, you could download some different versions from the website www.christusrex.org. It has the Lord's Prayer in hundreds of different languages!

Here's a text message version for mobile phones by Matthew Campbell from a competition on the Ship of Fools website:

dad@hvn,urspshl.we want wot u want&urth2b like hvn.giv us food&4giv r sins lyk we 4giv uvaz.don't test us!save us!bcos we kno ur boss, ur tuf&ur cool 4 eva!ok?

Here's a pidgin English version from Hawaii:

God, you our Fadda. You stay in da sky. We like all da peopo know fo shua how you stay, and dat you good and spesho inside, an we like dem give you plenny respeck.
We like you come king ova hea now.
We like everybody make jalike you like, ova hea inside da world, jalike da angel guys up inside da sky make jalike you like.
Give us da food we need fo every day.
Let us go, an throw out our shame fo all da bad kine stuff we do to you, jalike us gys let da odda guys go awready, an we no stay huhu wit dem fo all da kine bad stuff dey do to us.
No let us get chance fo do bad kine stuff, but take us outa dea, so da Bad Guy no can hurt us. Cuz you our king, you got da real power, an you stay awesome fo eva.
Dass it!

Here's another version.

Dearest Dad
You're far bigger than we can imagine and right near to us at the same time. Help us to remember your bigness alongside your closeness. Let your bigness come into every situation here on earth and let your nearness influence everyone so that our little earth will be like your great heaven.

Please give us what we need to live day by day. And forgive us when we do wrong, so we know you'll help us forgive those who do wrong to us. And guide us in good ways away from what will hurt us. And when we go wrong, rescue us. For everything is yours and always has been and always will be and that's how it should be.

Rap the Lord's Prayer

Ask the group if they can devise a catchy rap beat for saying the Lord's Prayer. A drum machine will certainly keep your technophiles happy. If you haven't got access to one, finger clicking and stamping are good.

Quiz on the Lord's Prayer

You could hold this quiz to recap what you've learnt over the whole course. A prize for everyone taking part might be a card with the Lord's Prayer written on it, or a picture of Dürer's *Praying Hands*.

You may want to adapt these questions to suit your children.

1. **Who invented the Lord's Prayer?**
    A) Moses
    B) Matthew
    C) Jesus

2. **Who asked Jesus how to pray?**
    A) His friends
    B) The Pharisees
    C) A reporter from *Galilean News*

3. **What are the opening words of the Lord's Prayer?**
    A) My Father
    B) Our Father
    C) Your Father

4. **The word Jesus uses in this first line is 'Abba'. What English word is this most like?**
    A) Oy you
    B) Daddy
    C) Honourable Father

5. **What does 'hallowed' mean?**
    A) Holy or set apart
    B) Hollow
    C) Greetings

6. **Give an example of hallowing God's name.**

7. **'Your kingdom come': Can you think of a parable about the kingdom of heaven?**

8. **'Your will be done': Where was Jesus when he prayed 'But do what you want and not what I want'?**
    A) By the river Jordan
    B) In the garden of Gethsemane
    C) At Mary and Martha's house

9. **Can you name a time when it might be hard to do what God wants rather than what you want?**

10. **Which of these is something you need?**
    A) Bread
    B) Sticky toffee pudding
    C) Burgers

11. **What might 'Give us today our daily bread' be changed to in China, where they don't eat bread much?**
    A) Give us today our daily fish and chips
    B) Give us today our daily crispy fried wan tun
    C) Give us today our daily rice

12. **Fill in the missing word in this part of the prayer: '............. us our sins'.**

13. **How many times does Jesus say we should forgive someone who sins against us?**
    A) Loads and loads and loads of times
    B) Once
    C) Not at all

14. **Name one thing that might tempt us.**

15. **What does 'deliver me' mean in the prayer?**
    A) Send me a letter
    B) Rescue me
    C) Remove my liver

16. **True or false: Jesus didn't put 'For the kingdom, the power and the glory are yours, now and for ever. Amen' at the end of his prayer.**

17. **What does 'Amen' mean?**
    A) I trust you'll answer this prayer
    B) At last the prayer's over
    C) That's all, folks

Act the Lord's Prayer

Ask the group to split into pairs and practise a short sketch between two puppets or actors. One of them doesn't understand the Lord's Prayer and the other one wants to help him understand.

Sign up to the Lord's Prayer

You'll need pens, sealing wax and seals—coins of different sorts, initial stampers, embossed rings and so on— and a copy of the Lord's Prayer on card.

Say that when you say 'Amen' at the end of the prayer, it's like saying that you personally believe God will answer this prayer. Tell the group about the way kings would put their seal on letters to prove that they were genuine signatures. Invite the children to show that they believe God will answer their prayer by reading out the prayer together, then signing their names and pressing the seal of their choice into the warm wax blobs that you make on the bottom of the copy of the Lord's Prayer.

Thread the Lord's Prayer

In the story right at the start of this book, Jesus' words are described as jewels, each falling into just the right place to make a beautiful necklace. For centuries, Catholics have used rosaries to help them remember their prayers. You could encourage the children to make a Lord's Prayer necklace, key ring or bracelet.

You'll need different sizes and shapes of beads, fastenings from a craft or sewing shop, strong thread or wire, key rings if required.

Ask the children to choose a bead to represent each phrase of the Lord's Prayer and to thread them together to make a necklace, bracelet, key ring or similar.

Now you can all say the prayer together, counting the beads as you go along.

Make space for the Lord's Prayer

It's appropriate to finish the book with this activity, as this is how the whole project started. Here is a *Godly Play* version of the Lord's Prayer, based on a script by Sue Doggett.

If you've used *Godly Play*, you'll know the technique. If you haven't, it's very easy! Just follow the instructions as you go along. Basically, you're laying the felt squares on top of the underlay to make a multi-coloured line and placing the symbols on top of the appropriate square.

Keep all your movements slow, gentle and reverent. Take your time: giving the group space

LEADER

GREEN	BLACK	RED	YELLOW	PURPLE	GREY	BLUE	WHITE

        CHILDREN

for listening to God is all part of the process. Keep your eye contact on the materials; don't look at your audience until the prayer is finished. This is an important principle of *Godly Play*. You should find that your audience's eyes will be on the materials too, rather than you, so that you 'disappear' and allow the prayer to tell its own story. For this reason, you will need at least one other adult sitting with the group to maintain discipline gently if needed, without your having to interrupt the flow of the prayer to attend to an individual within the group.

You'll need an underlay of cream or oatmeal-coloured fabric measuring approximately 15cm x 120cm, and eight small squares of felt measuring approximately 15cm x 15cm, in green, black, red, yellow, purple, grey, blue and white. The underlay needs to fit under the felt squares exactly when they are laid end to end upon it.

If you wish to give the underlay more substance, you will need to cut the fabric to twice the width plus seam allowances (approximately 33cm) and add 3cm to the length. Sew a seam down the long ends and one short end. Turn inside out and press with an iron, neatly turning the raw edges of the open end under as you go. Slip-stitch the open edge.

The underlay then needs to be loosely rolled, ready to be unrolled just enough to accept each new square of felt as the prayer unfolds. Through-out the prayer, you will be unrolling just enough for each square to be added at the appropriate time. Remember that your audience needs to read the prayer left to right, so everything has to be the right way round and the right way up for them, not for you. You will need to practise this beforehand by laying everything out and then going round to the other side of the cloth to see how everything looks from your audience's point of view. Adjust as necessary!

The artefacts for each part of the prayer might include:

- a model hen and chicks
- a nightlight in a small holder (and matches)
- four red hearts
- a small bread roll
- a gold heart
- a stone
- a rainbow
- red feathers
- a triangle of orange felt measuring 15cm x 15cm x 21 cm (i.e. half a felt square)
- a small crown made of gold card
- a small glass bowl, bubble mixture and blower

All the artefacts need to be placed in a large shoebox which has been painted gold. Practise beforehand arranging the artefacts in the best order for each item to be to hand as you need it. This will save you scrabbling around in the box, looking for an item, when you unfold the prayer with your group. The felt squares need to be stacked in order, with the green square on the top of the pile and the white on the bottom so that they are in the correct order for use.

Of course you may want to substitute your own symbols and visuals. Perhaps you have been inspired by the objects chosen by the children in the 'quiet space' activities. or you might just have different ideas that mean more to you. For example, Sue uses a sheep and shepherd with the green square instead of my hen and chicks.

NB: Whenever you use a candle or nightlight on your cloth, do take care to observe safety precautions. The children love to light the candle for you after the first telling of the prayer. This can be done with responsible children under super-vision, but never let children light candles un-supervised. If you wish to use a nightlight or candle, always place it in a holder to prevent wax spillage from spoiling your materials and, for the same reason, always allow the wax to set before putting the candles or nightlights back into the box.

The script

Start the session with all the materials for the prayer in the shoebox, which is placed just to the side of you, within easy reach. Settle down and feel the prayer gathering inside you before you begin. Then begin by saying:

'Prayer is a golden gift from God...'

(Draw the shoebox to the front of you and trace the shape of the lid with your finger.)

'This box is gold in colour. I wonder if it contains anything about prayer? ... Jesus knew all about prayer... He prayed early in the morning... he prayed late into the night... he prayed for his friends... and for those who would have counted themselves his enemies... He prayed for little children... he laid his hand upon them and he blessed them...

'One day, when Jesus was praying, his friends came up to him and said, "Lord, teach us to pray." ... I wonder if this box can tell us more about the prayer that Jesus taught his friends? Shall we open the lid and see what's inside?'

(Open the box, leaving the lid propped against it so that it obscures the contents from your audience, and take out the underlay. Unroll it just enough to allow you to place your first square of felt on to it.)

'Remember that God your heavenly Father is better than the best parent you could ever imagine. He cares for you so much that he wants you to call him "Abba"—"Daddy". He loves you even more than a mother hen loves her chicks.'

(Place the hen and chicks on the felt.)

'So, when you pray, start your prayer like this... Abba ... our father in heaven...'

(Unroll the underlay just enough to accept the second felt square and place the black felt alongside the green felt. Place the nightlight on it and light the wick.)

'And remember when you pray that your heavenly father is very holy. He is all that is good... all that is light... hallowed—holy—be your name...'

(Unroll the underlay just enough to accept the third felt square and place the red felt alongside the black felt.)

'Your heavenly father loves you so much that he has spread his love to every corner of the world... north... south ... east... west...'

(Place the four hearts one by one on the red felt.)

'There is no part of the world that your heavenly father doesn't care for... there is no part of the world that he doesn't want us to care for... Your kingdom come... your will be done... on earth as it is in heaven.

'Your heavenly father loves you so much that he wants you to have every good thing you need... He'd give those things to us anyway... but he loves us to ask for the things we need... he loves us to share our lives with him... Give us this day our daily bread.'

(Unroll the underlay just enough to accept the fourth felt square and place the yellow felt alongside the red felt. Place the bread on it.)

'Our daily bread is not just the toast we have for breakfast... or the honey sandwich we have for tea. No, it's everything we need… our friends… our families… our homes… clothes to keep us warm… food and love to nourish us… Give us today our daily bread…'

(Unroll the underlay just enough to accept the fifth felt square and place the purple felt alongside the yellow felt. Place the gold heart on it.)

'This part of the prayer is all about God's love for us… but he knows that we don't always get things right… and he has given us ten best ways to help us live, to help us know when we get things wrong… Forgive us our sins…

'And God wants us to love as we are loved… to forgive those who sin against us… This part of the prayer is about what we can do for others…'

(Unroll the underlay just enough to accept the sixth felt square and place the grey felt alongside the purple felt. Place the stone on it.)

'God knows that there are things that make us stumble and fall… there are grey areas when we are not sure whether we are doing right or wrong… Perhaps there are times when we know that we are doing wrong… but we want to do that thing all the same…'

(Lay the rainbow over the stone.)

'… Lead us not into temptation… but deliver us from evil… God has given us the sign of the rainbow to remind us that he will never, ever turn his back on us… he will never, ever let us go…'

(Pause and then run your finger along the side of the prayer that is so far unfolded.)

'This is the part of the prayer that you will find in your Bible. But today the end of the prayer praises God for his eternal love…'

(Unroll the underlay just enough to accept the seventh felt square and place the blue felt alongside the grey felt.)

'… Yours is the kingdom…'

(Lay the orange felt triangle over one half of the blue square.)

'… the power…'

(Lay the red feathers on top of the orange triangle.)

'… and the glory…'

(Lay the gold crown on the blue triangle shape.)

'… from the beginning of time… with us today… for ever and ever…'

(Unroll the underlay completely to accept the eighth felt square and place the white felt alongside the blue felt. Place the glass dish containing the bubble mixture and blower on it.)

'… Amen.'

(Blow bubbles into the air towards your audience.)

Look up. Pause and then say, 'Shall we say the prayer together?'

Slowly repeat the prayer, gently touching each artefact as each phrase of the prayer is prayed. As you say 'Amen', blow bubbles into the air once more.

Concluding the prayer

You could follow the prayer with wondering questions, or just use it to close your session. When you have finished, carefully put the artefacts away in reverse order. Children love to be invited to (gently!) blow out the candle. When the artefacts have been returned to the box, pile the felt squares carefully in reverse order, starting with the white felt, and put them into the box. Finally, carefully roll up the underlay and place that in the box, too. Put the lid back on the box and draw the box back to the starting position by your side.

Act the Lord's Prayer

Here's a child-friendly version of a script that seems to be in the public domain on the internet—my apologies if the original idea belongs to someone.

Prayer goes both ways

SAM: Our Father in heaven…

GOD: Hello!

SAM: Sssh, I'm praying.

GOD: I know. I'm listening.

SAM: Oh. You're… God, then? But I'm only saying the Lord's Prayer. It's not like I'm expecting an answer.

GOD: But this is one of my all-time favourites! Go on.

SAM: OK, Lord, if you say so. Hallowed be your name…

GOD: Yes, please. That would be a nice change from being used as a swear word.

SAM: Your kingdom come, your will be done on earth as it is in heaven…

GOD: Which bit of earth?

SAM: Well, foreign countries, I suppose.

GOD: What about your bit of earth? Your home, your school, your football club? Are you asking that my kingdom should come there as well?

SAM: Your kingdom come in my school? I don't see how that could happen.

GOD: You also prayed, 'Your will be done.' Perhaps that's your answer. If you start doing what you know I want—looking after Joshua at playtime when everyone else ignores him…

letting yourself get excited about my beautiful number patterns in numeracy instead of daydreaming… opening your mind and your heart to the wonderful world you live in, through your studies… all these sorts of thing… perhaps then my kingdom will come even in Wall Street Primary School.

SAM: It's only a prayer!

GOD: Careful, Sam, or I might answer it…

SAM: You can answer the next bit! Give us today our daily bread.

GOD: Certainly. But it wouldn't hurt to lay off the daily chocolate and crisps occasionally. And don't forget, you need more than just food to keep you going.

SAM: And forgive us our sins…

GOD: Anything in particular?

SAM: Oh God. I hoped you wouldn't ask. I've been feeling a bit guilty about a few things. Like shouting at my mum. And copying off Harry in the test. And laughing at Janey when she hurt herself in the playground. Sorry, God.

GOD: That's fine, Sam. Thank you for telling me. I've forgotten it all already. I know you feel better. But you haven't quite finished this part...

SAM: Asweforgivethosewhosinagainstus... Yes yes, I know I should. But you don't know what it's like when your sister is such a pain!

GOD: I had sisters. And brothers. And friends. And enemies. And a mum and dad who could all be frustrating at times, even when I loved them very much. Now you've been forgiven yourself, don't you want to forgive the people who hurt you too?

SAM: It's very hard, God!

GOD: I know. It really hurts to forgive someone. But that's why you're praying about it—so that I can help you. Just like in the next bit of the Lord's Prayer.

SAM: OK... I forgive my sister. Ooof.

GOD: Excellent! Go on.

SAM: And lead us not into temptation but deliver us from evil. Yeah, I'm not too keen on evil if it's anything like when I watched that creepy video

Evil Bloodsucking Tentacles from Planet Terror round at Mike's house when his mum was out... that was scary.

GOD: Oh yes. I'll certainly look after you. But you can help out. When Mike tells you to watch videos with '18' on them, you could always say 'No'. Common sense, Sam. We're in this together.

SAM: The end of the prayer's pretty good. For the kingdom, the power and the glory are yours, now and for ever, Amen.

GOD: Thank you, I appreciate that.

SAM: Good. I guess that's why I pray the Lord's Prayer really—sometimes I haven't got the words for what I want to say. And I know you like this one.

GOD: Yes I do. Very much. And Sam?

SAM: Yes, Lord?

GOD: I like you very much too.

Ongoing wall display

This session shows a beautiful bead necklace, bracelet or wristband. You will find the template on page 127.

 Reproduced with permission from *The Lord's Prayer Unplugged* published by BRF 2004 (978 1 84101 262 9)

Bible Index

Appendix

Church family tree

Number one prayers

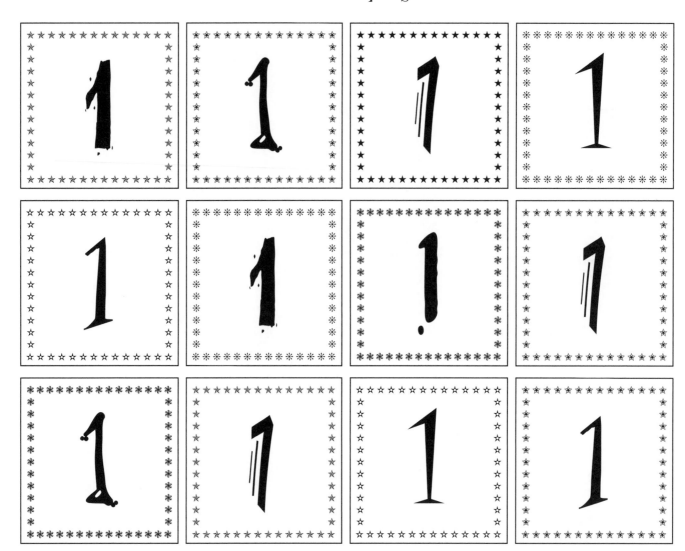

What's in a name?

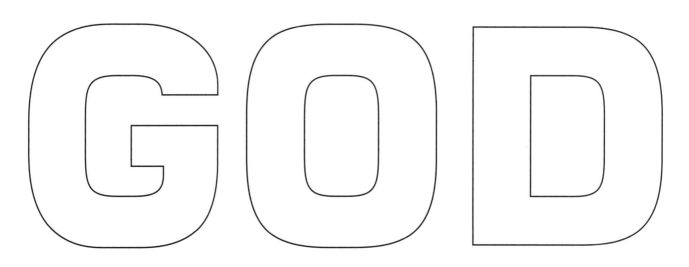

Kingdom parable

Psalm 51:1–12

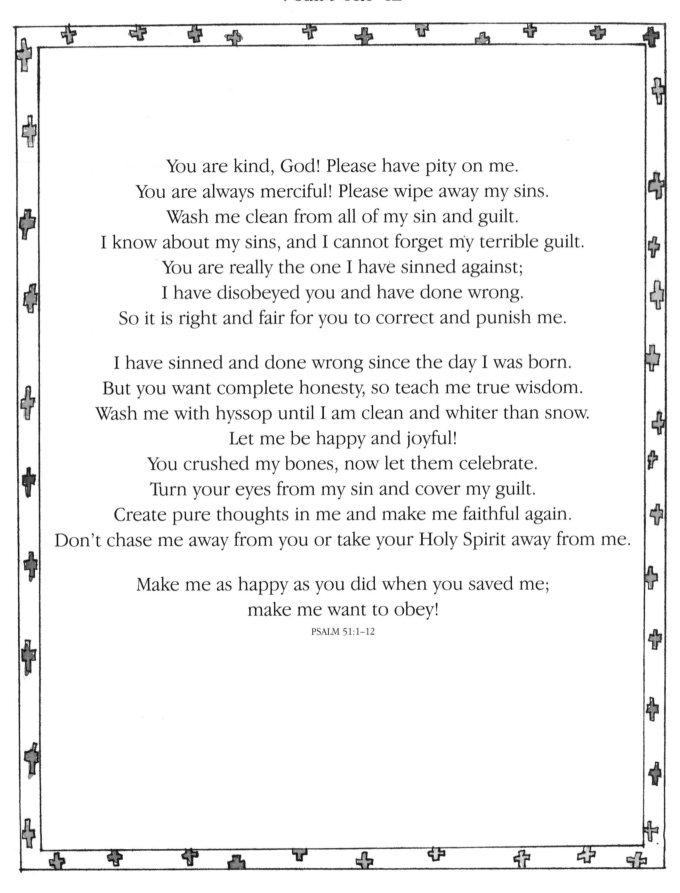

You are kind, God! Please have pity on me.
You are always merciful! Please wipe away my sins.
Wash me clean from all of my sin and guilt.
I know about my sins, and I cannot forget my terrible guilt.
You are really the one I have sinned against;
I have disobeyed you and have done wrong.
So it is right and fair for you to correct and punish me.

I have sinned and done wrong since the day I was born.
But you want complete honesty, so teach me true wisdom.
Wash me with hyssop until I am clean and whiter than snow.
Let me be happy and joyful!
You crushed my bones, now let them celebrate.
Turn your eyes from my sin and cover my guilt.
Create pure thoughts in me and make me faithful again.
Don't chase me away from you or take your Holy Spirit away from me.

Make me as happy as you did when you saved me;
make me want to obey!

PSALM 51:1–12

The worst place to be

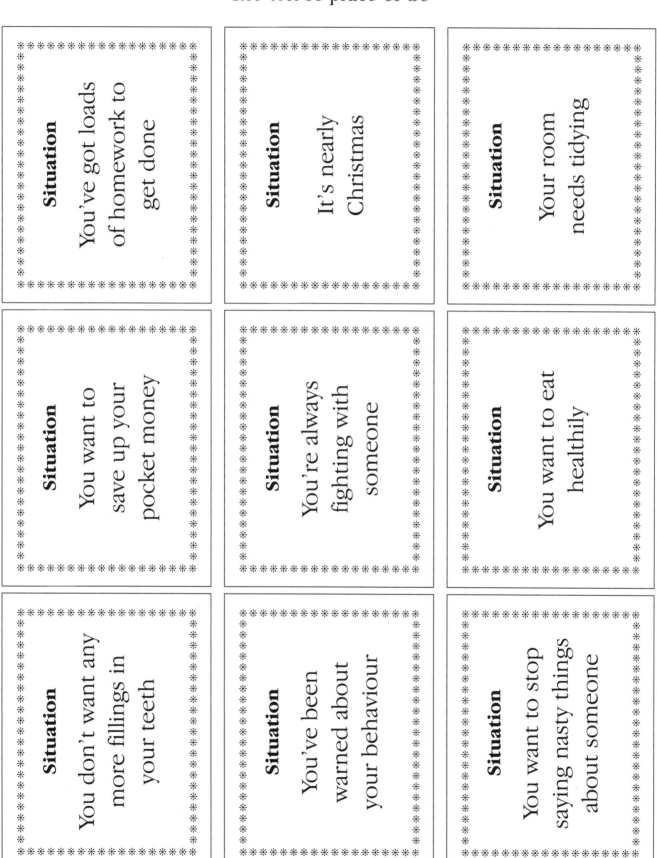

Situation
You've got loads of homework to get done

Situation
It's nearly Christmas

Situation
Your room needs tidying

Situation
You want to save up your pocket money

Situation
You're always fighting with someone

Situation
You want to eat healthily

Situation
You don't want any more fillings in your teeth

Situation
You've been warned about your behaviour

Situation
You want to stop saying nasty things about someone

The worst place to be

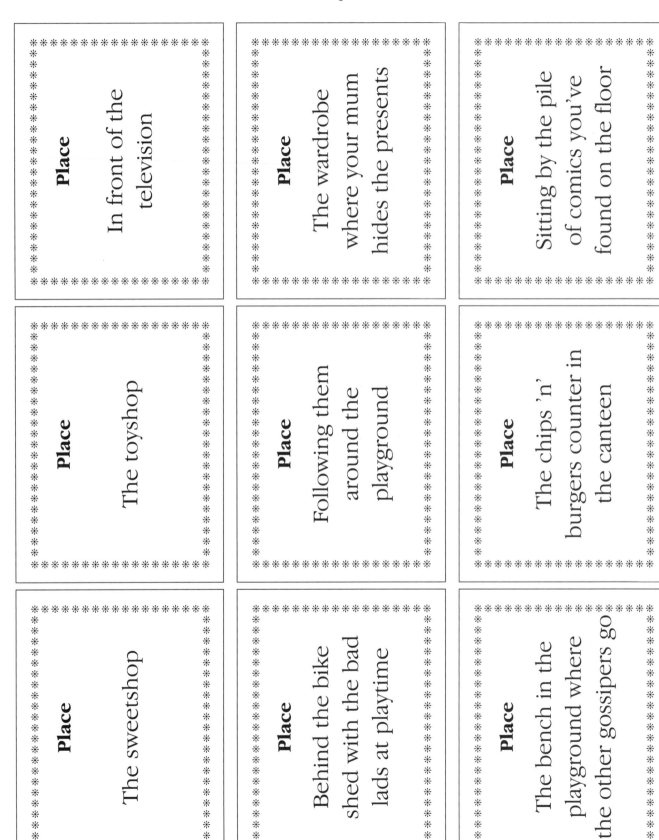

Place

In front of the television

Place

The wardrobe where your mum hides the presents

Place

Sitting by the pile of comics you've found on the floor

Place

The toyshop

Place

Following them around the playground

Place

The chips 'n' burgers counter in the canteen

Place

The sweetshop

Place

Behind the bike shed with the bad lads at playtime

Place

The bench in the playground where the other gossipers go

Resurrection

Sound

Time in seconds

Psalm 23

❶

You, Lord, are my shepherd. I will never be in need.

❷

You let me rest in fields of green grass.

❸

You lead me to streams of peaceful water, and you refresh my life.

❹

You are true to your name, and you lead me along the right paths.

❺

I may walk through valleys as dark as death, but I won't be afraid. You are with me, and your shepherd's rod makes me feel safe.

❻

You treat me to a feast, while my enemies watch.

❼

You honour me as your guest, and you fill my cup until it overflows.

❽

Your kindness and love will always be with me each day of my life, and I will live for ever in your house, Lord.

Flickbook

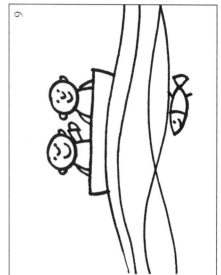

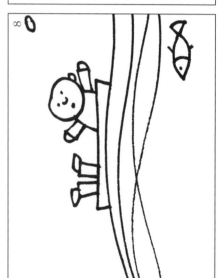

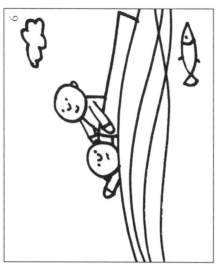

Draw the Lord's Prayer

❶

Our Father in heaven

❷

Hallowed be your name

❸

Your kingdom come

❹

Your will be done on earth
as in heaven.

❺

Give us today our daily bread

❻

And forgive us our sins as we
forgive those who sin against us.

❼

Lead us not into temptation

❽

But deliver us from evil.

❾

For the kingdom, the power and the
glory are yours, now and for ever.
Amen

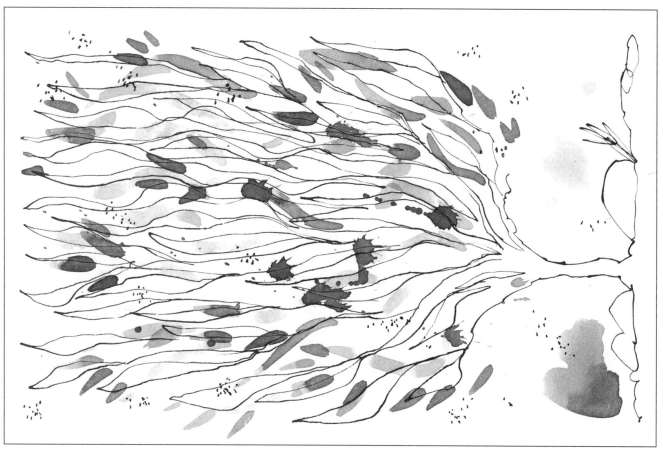

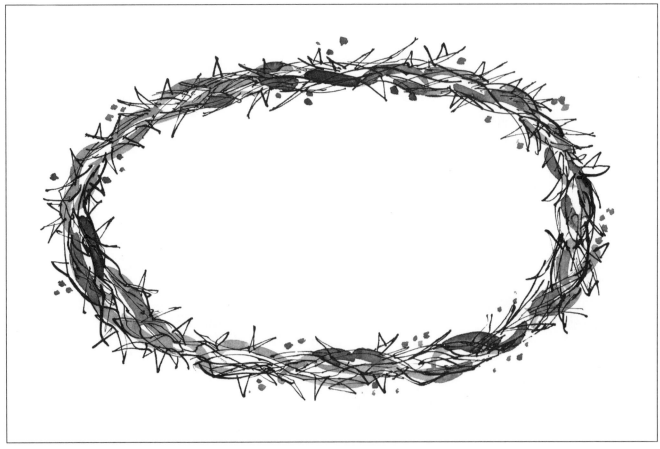

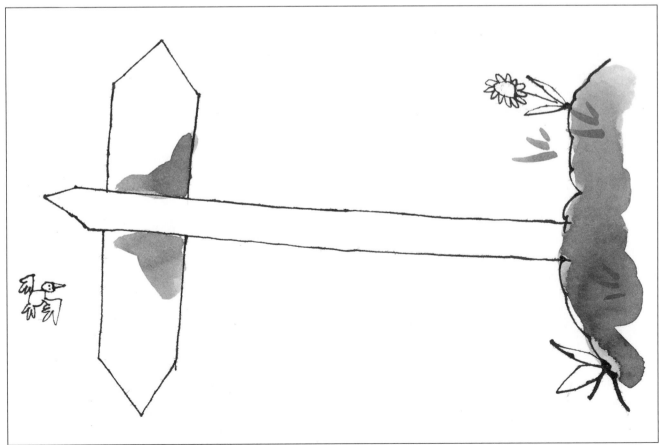

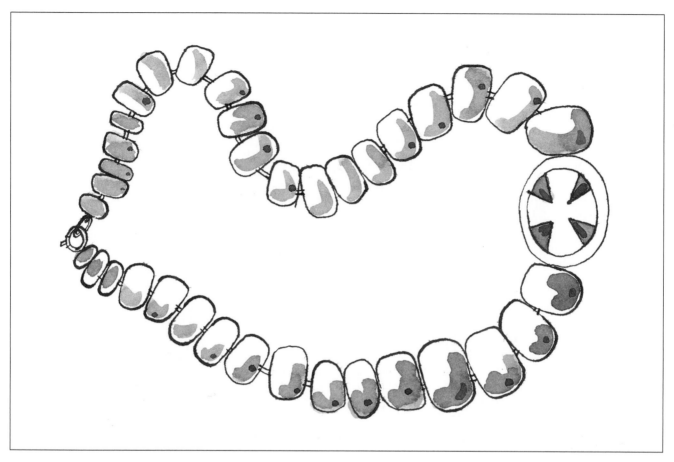

★ ★ ★ ★ ★ ★

OTHER RESOURCES FROM BARNABAS

REF 978 1 84101 243 8, £12.99

Ideal for busy teachers and church leaders who have endless demands on their time and energy and need stories that jump off the page, into the imagination and, from there, into daily life.

Drawn from all four Gospels, the pieces are 'unplugged' in that they get to the heart of the biblical text, reflecting the life of Jesus in action: who he is, what he said and what he did. Some tell the story, some explore an aspect of the original account. Many pieces include children. Some pieces are meant to be performed, some to be enjoyed quietly; but the overall aim is to have fun and enjoy unplugging the Gospels!